Darien
•

Midway
○

Sunbury

Sapelo

St. Catherines

Ossabaw

The Sea
Islands of
Georgia

Y SYSTEM
Library

D1159977

By Betsy Fancher

THE LOST LEGACY OF GEORGIA'S GOLDEN ISLES
BLUE RIVER

THE LOST LEGACY OF
Georgia's Golden Isles

THE LOST LEGACY OF

Georgia's

BETSY FANCHER

Golden Isles

Photographs by PETER HUDSON

DOUBLEDAY & COMPANY, INC.
GARDEN CITY, NEW YORK
1971

Introduction adapted from "The Georgia Coast Where the Tides of History Wash on the Shore" which appeared in the June 1969 issue of *Southern Living;* copyright 1969 by The Progressive Farmer Company.

The chapters on Gullah and the Sea Islands adapted from articles which appeared in the May 1969 and December 1969 issues of *Atlanta,* respectively; copyright 1969 by the Atlanta Chamber of Commerce.

The chapter on The Cloister (Sea Island) adapted from an article which appeared in the November 1968 issue of *Atlanta;* copyright 1968 by the Atlanta Chamber of Commerce.

The chapter on Cumberland adapted from "Georgia Sea Island That Slumbers Like a Time Capsule" which appeared in the May 1970 issue of *Holiday.*

DESIGNED BY EARL TIDWELL

Library of Congress Catalog Card Number 79–133621
Copyright © 1970, 1971 by Betsy Fancher
All Rights Reserved
Printed in the United States of America

For my daughters—Laurie, Amelia, and Martha

Preface

The author is deeply indebted to the many people who contributed to this book—their reminiscences and experiences, their private collections of out-of-print books, their family scrapbooks, letters, journals, their friendship, help, and encouragement.

The idea was born with Miss Faith Brunson, whose constant support and encouragement finally brought the book into being. The historical research of Miss Bessie Lewis, the knowledgeable historian of Pine Harbor, Georgia, has been an invaluable source of material. So has the library of the late Margaret Davis Cate at Fort Frederica on St. Simons Island and the Georgia Historical Society in Savannah, where Miss Lila Hawes was a great help. Of great value too were the private collections of Ross Ingram and Jim Whitnel, of Atlanta; Alfred Jones, of Sea Island; my aunt, Mrs. Charlton Theus, of Savannah; Mildred Huie, of St. Simons Island; Ewald Kockritz, of Miami, who was of particular help; and Mrs. Clifford West, who heads the Ossabaw Island Project, which offered the author the leisure and solitude not only to work but to become more intimately acquainted with the magic of the islands.

Dr. Eugene Odum, Director of the Institute of Ecology at the University of Georgia was of great assistance, as were Dr. James Henry, Director of the University of Georgia Marine Institute at Sapelo Island and the other scientists there; Robert Hanie, who heads the Georgia Natural Areas Council; and O. R. Ferguson, Sam Candler, and Bob Rischarde of Cumberland Island.

On St. Simons Island, those who helped along the way include Eugenia Price, Joyce Blackburn, Donald S. McClain, Sig Kaufman, Mildred Wilcox, Don Everett, Lloyd Benjamin, and May Corb of the Shore Bird book shop, and folksinger Bessie Jones and her family. On Sea Island there was Helen Casky; on Jekyll, Horace Caldwell and Tallu Fish; on Hilton Head, Ralph Hilton; and so many others, more than I could possibly name. I am deeply indebted to Ashby Tucker, of Atlanta, for her help in putting the manuscript in final form, and to my husband Jim and my three daughters for their encouragement and forbearance.

Contents

Contents

Introduction

Ever since 1562, when Jean Ribaut, the adventurous French Huguenot, described the Georgia coast as the "fairest, fruitfullest and pleasantest of all the world" it has been a "debatable land."

During the seventeenth century, France, Spain, and England vied for the coast in a series of bloody forays that culminated in Oglethorpe's decisive victory at the Battle of Bloody Marsh on St. Simons Island in 1742. Today this is still an embattled land, coveted by industrialists, by real estate developers, and by conservationists who believe that its solitary beaches, its bearded forests and vast, grieving salt marshes hold a dimension of wildness essential to the human heart.

For all its pervasive sense of history, its crumbling forts, its overgrown plantation ruins, and the aching poetry of its moss-shrouded graveyards, this is still virgin territory. Preserved by poverty, by neglect and by isolation, it has escaped the bulldozer and the developer. The twentieth century has made few inroads here. A visit to the Georgia coast is like a journey back in time, a pilgrimage to regain the squandered legacy of beauty, history, and sea wilderness irrevocably lost to most Americans.

Even in Savannah, the burgeoning doorway to the coast, the past is scrupulously preserved. Restorations range from the grill-fretted row houses on St. Julien Street to the freshly laid brick walkways in Johnson Square, from the little jewel-like parks along the waterfront to the blurred tombstones in Bonaventure Cemetery.

Below Savannah, the traveler on U.S. 17 is in Gullah country, a region of ancient superstitions, intricate rituals, and a primitive language of pure poetry. It is marked only by little shacks with windows painted blue to ward off haunts and a few overgrown graveyards scarred with broken pottery— a Gullah symbol of the brokenness of life.

The spire of Midway Church soars improbably amid the pine barrens at the turn-off to the haunted road to Sunbury, the dead town that was once an important colonial port. Known as the "Cradle of Liberty," the little Congregationalist church was the center of St. John's parish which produced two signers of the Declaration of Independence, four Georgia governors, six foreign missionaries, and eighty-two ministers—many of them buried in the walled cemetery, beneath furred tombstones whose faded lyrics testify, "Lo!

where this silent marble weeps, a friend, a husband, father sleeps . . ."

Just below Darien, founded by the Scottish Highlanders in the eighteenth century, you can see the solitary chimneys of the lime kiln on Butler's Island, where the great English actress Fanny Kemble wrote her bitter *Journal of a Residence on a Georgian Plantation*, a book said to have sparked English sentiment against the slaveholders, perhaps ultimately determining the defeat of the Confederacy.

The traveler in this country of praline signs and peacock bedspreads sees nothing of the offshore islands which Sir Robert Montgomery named the Golden Islands when he envisioned them as the baronial Margravate of Azilia in 1717. St. Catherine's Island was the site of one of the nation's first Franciscan monasteries where Spanish priests taught the Creek Indians as early as 1566. Two centuries later it was the home of the enigmatic Button Gwinnett, Georgia signer of the Declaration of Independence, whose rare signature is valued at $15,000 today. The occasional visitor can still see the cabins once occupied by the freed slaves who, under a Negro headwaiter, Tunis Campbell, set up the headquarters for a black separatist nation here after the Civil War.

Ossabaw Island's proud, pink stucco mansion now houses philosophers, poets, painters, musicians and scientists—creative thinkers of every persuasion who, savoring the sensitive hospitality of the Ossabaw Island Project, are producing everything from best-selling novels to fine paintings.

Sapelo, once the home of the pioneer of Sea Island cotton, Thomas Spalding, is now being used as a vast outdoor laboratory by the Marine Institute of the University of Georgia, which is pioneering basic research in the ecology of the marshlands. And Cumberland, with its long, lovely beaches and matted forests, may soon be designated a national seashore.

The insular life can best be savored at St. Simons, at Jekyll Island, or at Sea Island. Some prefer Jekyll with its comfortable, unpretentious motels, its fine golf courses, its amusement park, and its wide beaches scarred with gaunt and skeletal oaks. Deer flit across the patios of new split-level houses and roam the patterned gardens of abandoned gingerbread houses once owned by the Cranes, the Rockefellers and the J. P. Morgans, when this was the province of the legendary millionaires' club. Today little remains of the slave era but the empty tombs of the DuBignon family, who owned the island when the slave ship *Wanderer* landed here in 1858 with the nation's last illegal cargo of slaves.

Searchers after the lost legacy would do better to explore St. Simons, the largest of the coastal islands. The great plantations owned by the coastal aristocrats in the golden era of Sea Island cotton now lend their stately names to new housing developments, and the fields and marshes of Blackbanks have been transformed into a popular new resort club. But the island has lost little of its pervasive sense of history. At the Harlem Road Church of God, visitors can still see the worshipers doing the holy dances and hear the "shouts" first sung by native Africans in the praise houses of the coastal rice plantations. Frederica, the fort which Oglethorpe built to defend the Southern frontier against possible attack from the Spanish, has been preserved as a national monument— visitors can still see the plots of the dead town where three hundred English tradesmen settled in 1736. The gilded, undulating marsh grasses, once crimsoned by the blood of a hundred Spanish dead, has changed little since the Battle of Bloody Marsh.

The ghosts of St. Simons range from the Ebo slaves who drowned themselves in Dunbar Creek in a mute, hopeless protest against slavery, to Mary the Wanderer, who rides a white stallion down the moss-canopied island roads in search of the lover who perished in a boating accident a century ago. Islanders accept them amiably as reassuring proof of the continuity of life, a natural consequence of living with history.

St. Simons itself challenges the traveler's concept of time. Oglethorpe seems very real when the tourist can sip a fine wine at the Sea Island Yacht Club overlooking the bluff where the English troops first landed. At the two-million-dollar Methodist Center, a shrine to John Wesley, the founder of Methodism, you can hear a sermon on the death of God near the site where Wesley preached to the "murderous, gluttonous Indians" in a ministry which later was to end in a bitter scandal in Savannah. And you can savor the shrimp mull at The Deck while sharing an expansive view of the Marshes of Glynn. "'Tis here, 'tis here thou canst unhand thy heart and Breathe it free," Sidney Lanier wrote in 1880.

The traveler who crosses the St. Simons causeway, through the shivering, sun-gilded marshes, may well share the same expansiveness of heart. This is not a journey to be lightly made. For the traveler is apt to recover, on any of the coastal islands, not only his lost legacy of history and wilderness, but his own squandered spirit.

THE LOST LEGACY OF
Georgia's Golden Isles

1

Savannah

A RENAISSANCE OF THE HEART

On Founders Day, when tourists from all over the nation flock to Savannah's waterfront to relive the high drama of Oglethorpe's landing in 1733 with a beleaguered company of English Protestants on the good ship *Ann*, the revelers in the city's nineteenth-century drawing rooms toast Savannah with Chatham Artillery punch in the same spirit of lyrical ardor with which their forebears toasted London, Dublin, and the Scottish Highlands.

Like Dublin, like London and Paris, Savannah is not so much a city as a region of the heart, a quality of grace and leisure that has almost vanished from urban life. Few American cities inspire the loyalties that Savannah engenders in both her visitors and her native sons. Her admirers have ranged from General James Oglethorpe who conceived her, to General Sherman, who ravished her, from the generation of Negro blues singers who mythologized her to the hard-headed financiers who cherished her through the bitter years of a prolonged depression. Somehow they preserved her ageless beauty and her unique life style. And today, when the cities which once obscured her are fighting for their lives, her admirers are gallantly ushering her into her finest hour as a prototype of the urban environment.

The city which Lady Astor once described as a beautiful woman with a dirty face is today a seductive and over-powering beauty. The overblown, azalea-splashed squares laid out by Oglethorpe in 1733, the grill-fretted row houses, the walled gardens, intricately patterned with camellias and boxwood, the waterfront with its torchlit restaurants and its dank, exotic little bistros, the moated forts and the moss-shrouded cemeteries with their immutable stone angels, the soul-deep blues of its Negro fishermen and the bourbon-and-branch-water conviviality of its old-line aristocracy have captivated a growing company of visitors. Among those now paying court to Savannah are city planners, environmentalists, industrial developers, poets, and artists—fugitives from urban blight and suburban sterility, who agree with the city's most open-handed benefactor, Atlanta banker Mills B. Lane, that Savannah is a city "where the good life is still possible."

Cars from every state in the union clog the narrow streets. Visitors to the Welcome Center are tripling every year, and at the bustling airport, where traffic is doubling, the moss-and-magnolia atmosphere crackles with brisk Yankee accents. The soft-voiced, blue-veined southern matriarchs who once bitterly debated the skyscraper dimensions of the new Desoto-Hilton are now complaining petulantly that it is simply not large enough and they've resigned themselves to the incongruities of the seven and a half million dollar Civic Center which combines, under one roof, a symphony hall, a sports arena and convention facilities.

Although the city's economy has long been solidly grounded on heavy industry and shipping, several nights a week officials of the Chamber of Commerce take groups of out-of-state industrialists on twilight tours of the port, citing the new deep-water industrial sites on moss-draped Hutchinson's Island, where Georgia's first slaves once toiled in the rice fields to support a Methodist orphanage ironically named Bethesda, "House of Mercy." Some of Savannah's newcomers, Grumman Aircraft for instance, are expanding rapidly, a fact the soft-spoken promoters mention casually over tall bourbon drinks while sunset gilds the wake of the *Waving Girl*. They also point to the great dredges which are now deepening the channel to make Savannah the most modern and accessible port on the east coast. Savannah's shipping potential, they will tell you, is unlimited. But perhaps their most effective selling point is the Skidway Institute of Oceanography, a consortium of southern universities who have combined, under the broad umbrella of the Ocean Science Center of the Atlantic, to conduct applied research and ocean-centered industry on what was once Robert Roebling's famed Modena Plantation. The island, whose first settler, a benighted man named Mouse "was reduced so low that he had scarce clothes to cover him," has become the launching pad for a major assault on the most significant scientific frontier of the next decade—the sea.

Ironically, when other southern cities were fairly exploding in the sun of postwar affluence, Savannah was a sleepy, seedily picturesque little city, drifting in the backwaters of the twentieth century. Her hard-driving sons went north to make a living and pen nostalgic valentines to her fading charms; the great houses where Washington once feasted had slumped into crumbling slum dwellings, and drunken derelicts dozed amid the azaleas in the blowsy neglected little squares dominated by bronze statues of Revolutionary heroes. What changed her ebbing fortunes? If there is one answer, it would have to be Historic Savannah, the non-profit citizens' group which was born when an elderly gentlewoman named Anna Hunter rallied her friends to protest the demolition of the city market for a parking lot in 1957. While Miss Hunter failed to save the market place, she did succeed in launching a strong citizens' group to combat the destruction of the city's architectural heritage.

Under the leadership of investment counselor Lee Adler, Historic Savannah went into action so quickly and effectively that within months the disgruntled demolitionists were calling it Hysteric Savannah. From the beginning, they recognized what the nation's outstanding city planners are belatedly acknowledging—that Savannah, laid out in 1733, is "the best planned city in the country." In the era of the bulldozer, the skyscraper, and the superhighway, they returned to Oglethorpe's initial plan, realizing that Savannah's squares, originally intended as rallying points against Indian attack, were also effective fortresses against the great enemies of the twentieth century—air pollution, high population density, tension, and alienation. Around these open areas were some of the finest examples of Regency and Greek Revival architecture in the nation, but they were fast being torn down by demolitionists who marketed their Hermitage plantation "Savannah Gray" brick at ten cents apiece to suburban builders. Traffic engineers were eying the squares for through streets; urban developers wanted to clear the "slums" for office buildings, and most of the city fathers regarded downtown Savannah as fit only for business transactions—the good life lay beyond the city limits.

Today Adler can look with nostalgic good humor on the days when he was fighting the "Battle of the Savannah Grays" and trying to save some of the city's handsomest manses a scant thirty minutes before the demolitionists' hammer fell. For Historic Savannah has been an unqualified success. Most of the city's historic homes have been restored; the city's core of decaying colonial-era slums has been transformed into a showcase of eighteenth-century architecture, shuttered brick period pieces, fretted with magnificent iron filigree balconies, their pedigree discreetly identified on a small gold plaque by Historic Savannah. The most recent date back to the early nineteenth century. The oldest belongs to Jim Williams, who has rescued at least thirty homes from "the bulldozer and the architect," among them his own stunning home, built by a Rhode Island planter in 1796, a gambrel-roofed mansion which boasts a widow's walk and a riotous assortment of ghosts. Though they have been exorcised by the Episcopal Bishop of South Georgia, they are still active enough to bring some of the world's leading mediums, Dame Sybil Lee for one, scurrying across the Atlantic to conduct seances there.

Restoration proved to be the key to the tourist trade, as Adler had long argued to a conservative Chamber of Commerce which had contributed to Savannah's reputation as "the best kept secret in America." Today, Savannah shrewdly and aggressively woos tourists, most notably with its Founders Day pageant—a week-long festival of candlelight tours, peeping tours of the city's jewel-like walled gardens, *bals masques*, puppet shows, art and sculpture exhibits, book fairs, jazz festivals, and commemorative services in the city's historic sanctuaries, from lofty-columned Christ Church, originated in 1733, to the First African Baptist Church, the nation's oldest Negro congregation, which grew out of the martyrdom of the slave Andrew, who was publicly flogged with the cat-o'-nine-tails for preaching the gospel to Savannah's first slaves.

Savannah has had a high sense of pageantry since its inception, when its festivals ranged from the beery feasts of England's patron saint, St. George, to the Highlanders' Festival of St. Andrew. Today its Founders Day pageant, held on February 12, Georgia Day, rivals Mardi Gras and Gasparilla for sheer spectacle. What it lacks in authenticity, it gains in flamboyant showmanship and open-hearted, high-spirited chauvinism.

Announced by the thunder of cannon, Oglethorpe and his little band of thirty-five families—"a great number of unfortunate people," the colony's trustees described them—sail into port on Mills Lane's Spanish sailing vessel, the *Cruz del Sur*, a colorful but ironic stand-in for the British bark *Ann* whose passengers had been dispatched not only to settle the coastal wilderness but to form a frontier bulwark against the Spanish in St. Augustine. Trailing the *Cruz del Sur* is a flock of noisy tugs and sleek power boats, while on shore a clutch of jubilant teen-agers, costumed in feathers and bells,

[26]

re-enact the dance that one of the settlers, Thomas Causton, described as "Antick postures with a spread Fan of White Feathers in each hand as a token of friendship." At the dock are a magnificently feathered Tomochichi, chief of the Yamacraws, a refugee band of the Creeks, whose village was to be the site of Savannah, and a buckskin-clad Mary Musgrove, the beautiful half-breed princess who was to serve as Oglethorpe's interpreter to the Indians.

The festival culminates in a happy confrontation between Oglethorpe, the settlers, their spiritual mentor John Wesley, the founder of Methodism who actually arrived two years later on the *Symonds*, Mary Musgrove and Tomochichi, who presents Oglethorpe with a buffalo skin, repeating the formal little speech first delivered by the kindly chieftain in the name of the Creek nation in 1733. The buffalo skin, he pointed out with an exquisite sense of symbolism, "is adorned on the inside with the head and feathers of an eagle. . . . because the eagle is an emblem of speed and the buffalo of strength." He compared the English to a bird because they flew over the water, to a beast because nothing could withstand their strength. "The feathers of the eagle are soft and signify love; the buffalo skin is warm and signifies protection. Therefore I hope the English will love and protect their little families," said the Chief of the Yamacraws—"sober, judicious men, straight and strong, almost naked," Thomas Causton, the storekeeper, described them.

With this meeting of some of the most flamboyant, flawed, and courageous characters in history, assembled by fate on one of the most benevolent and ill-conceived experiments in the annals of British imperialism, the pageant ends. The crowd dispels and Savannah basks in the heady euphoria of her noble heritage. Only the city's courtly and reticent little band of historians understands the dreams that were shattered on the sandy soil of Savannah, dreams whose betrayal was to lead to the folly of slavery, states' rights, secession, the Civil War, and the lingering, hypnotic veneration of the past which the city, in its new Renaissance of the heart, is only now overcoming.

The great experiment was conceived when Oglethorpe, as a member of Parliament, visited the Fleet Street prison in 1728 and found the debtors there "loaded with irons and. . . . barbarously used," reports Georgia's first historian, Hugh McCall, who was Savannah's jail keeper. The military man turned statesman chairmanned a committee in the House of Commons to investigate Britain's jails and in 1729 presented a series of resolutions which led to a wide-scale prison reform. He also introduced a scheme for resettling debtors in Georgia where they might, according to McCall, "instead of being a burthen and a disgrace, be made beneficial to the nation." They were to establish a barrier against the Spanish to the south and the French to the west and enrich the imperial economy by producing silk and wine—a wildly implausible scheme, as there was only one agriculturist among the impoverished company of the *Ann*. As for the soil and climate of the coastal wilderness, the settlers and their benefactors knew little more than the lyrical description contained in a widely circulated pamphlet titled "A new and accurate Account of the Province of South Carolina and Georgia."

. . . . so Sweet the air, so moderate the clime
None sickly lives or dies before his time
Heavn' sure has kept this spot on earth uncurst
To show how all things were created first.

By nightfall of that first day, as the settlers pitched their tents on the bluff, Thomas Causton, the storekeeper who had marveled at the "noble, ancient and hoary" forest of oaks, was slapping sandflies and complaining that "every insect here is stronger than in England." Nevertheless, by February 9, Oglethorpe had already marked out the first square of a town plan that called for tythings of ten houses each and of woods of four tythings each where the settlers were to raise the white mulberry trees, the grapes, oranges, and olives nurtured in the Trustees Garden, probably the first agricultural experiment station in history.

But mulberry trees, olives, grapevines, and exotic plants "will not satisfye a man when he is hungry, nor cloathe him when he is naked," poor Mr. Mouse wrote the trustees from his settlement on Skidaway Island where his futile attempts at agriculture "almost broak my constitution with hard working and hard liveing."

The example of South Carolina flourishing on a slave economy deepened the discontent of the beleaguered settlers, who were convinced that Oglethorpe's ban against slavery was at the root of their poverty. They found the marshes mysteriously poisonous—during the summer months so many died of "Bloody Flux and convulsions" that Charles Wesley's disciple George Whitefield opened an orphanage for the colony's bereft children. While lawyers were barred from Georgia— "every man is his own lawyer," Oglethorpe had told them— discipline was strict. Dissolute women were scourged with sixty lashes of the cat-o'-nine-tails down Bull Street and one Robert Parker complained to the trustees that "I have seen a woman sit in the stocks for three hours when it rained hard (and the only Dairy wife we have to supply the colony with butter)." They railed about Oglethorpe's prohibition against rum, though he provided them with ample rations of strong beer, and they bridled under the spiritual tyranny of John Wesley complaining that his endless prayers, meetings and sermons kept them from their labors. Hugh McCall testified later that anyone who differed from his strange creed of "Methodism," was barred from worship services, "contrary to the spirit and tenderness authorized by the Christian religion." His Apostolic constitutions seemed "judiciously calculated to debase and depress the minds of the people and humble them with fastings, penances and drinking water." He was accused of dividing families, engaging spies in their homes and demanding to know not only the secret sins but even the dreams of the female parishioners.

Oglethorpe had his own problems. He made six trips across the Atlantic at his own expense to plead for more financial help from the trustees and to recruit new settlers. In 1734, Tomochichi, his wife and adopted son went with him to be presented at court. An old man, benevolent and wise, awed by the grandeur of the British court, he presented the king a clutch of eagle feathers. . . . "emblems of peace in our lands. . . . We have brought them over to leave them with you o great king, as a token of everlasting peace."

The destiny of the young colony was in Oglethorpe's hands. The Spaniards, with troops coming in from Havana, were planning a massive attack on the colony. Their emissaries were trying to spark an insurrection among South Carolina slaves and they were recruiting the Indians at Coweta, a move Oglethorpe stemmed with the help of Mary Musgrove at a formal meeting, solemnized by the "black drink" of cassina berries, in which the English were given St. Simons

Island, Cumberland, and Amelia, and the islands of St. Catherine's, Ossabaw, and Sapelo were reserved as hunting lands for the Indians.

By 1736 Oglethorpe had settled the Salzburgers, Protestant refugees from Bavaria, at Ebenezer, thirty miles north of Savannah. A company of Scottish Highlanders, noted for their courage and industry, was settled at Darien, sixty miles south of Savannah. The town of Frederica on St. Simons Island had been settled—"laid out with spacious streets. . . . margined with orange trees" and defended by "a pretty strong fort of tappy." Another fort was also built on the island and at Jekyll a brewery was established to supply ample rations of beer for the troops. Three batteries had been established on Cumberland, southernmost island in the chain, and Fort George was built at the mouth of the St. Johns River.

But this did not appease the malcontents. In 1738, while Oglethorpe, as commander in chief of the forces in South Carolina and Georgia, was in England recruiting a regiment to defend the frontiers of the colony, the Savannah free-holders, with the support of their magistrates, submitted a formal protest to the trustees saying that for all their "industry and application" they had not been able to raise sufficient produce to feed their families. Trade was impossible. "Carolina can raise everything that this colony can, and they, having their labor so much cheaper, will always ruin our market," they complained. They wanted free title so that their widows and daughters could inherit their land and, even more significantly, "the use of Negroes with proper limitations." If this were granted, Georgia would become "the most flourishing colony possessed by His Majesty in America." If it were refused, "we ourselves and families are not only ruined but even our posterity likewise."

When copies were sent to Reverend Boltzious, the spiritual leader at Ebenezer, the Germans drew up a counterposition asking quite practically for more of their countrymen, rather than slaves, and for some rice sieves from Charleston. The Highlanders took an impassioned stand against slavery in a petition from Darien.

"It is shocking to human nature that any race of mankind, and their posterity, should be sentenced to perpetual slavery; nor in justice can we think otherwise of it than that they are thrown amongst us to be our scourge one day or other for our sins; and as freedom to them must be as dear as to us, what a sense of horror it must bring about! And the longer it is unexecuted, the bloody scene must be the greater."

Hugh McCall later scoffed at the petition for slavery. He conceded that the land was poor, the swamps generated disease, and that of all the speculator's wild schemes, "silk and wine appear to have been the most delusive phantoms." But he maintained that the people of Savannah, having been "not only useless members, but burthensome to society at home, determined to be equally so abroad." He was also convinced that many of them had been lured to Georgia by false hopes kindled by the lyrical reports of John Wesley whose poem *Georgia* pictured the colony as a paradise "where all things into wild luxuriance ran and Burthen'd nature ask'd the aid of man. . . ."

The trustees staunchly defended Oglethorpe's stand against slavery. Moved by the petition from Darien, they rapped the magistrates for siding with the freeholders, declaring that "the surest foundations. . . . for the preservation of liberty and property" were "the laws against the use of slaves and for the entail of lands."

Oglethorpe was beset with problems that year. A group of Roman Catholic soldiers, of his own regiment, tried to assassinate him for spreading Protestanism in the colony. Georgia was threatened by South Carolina's Stono Rebellion, when South Carolina's slaves "hoisted their standards, proclaimed open rebellion" and, according to Hugh McCall, reduced the colony to "terror and consternation." War was declared against Spain in October 1739, and in May 1740 Oglethorpe launched an invasion of Florida with only 400 regular troops and returned months later in defeat, deathly ill with a fever, to find a pamphlet circulating about him by the malcontents deploring the absence of rum and slavery, comparing Georgia to an extinct civilization and ranking Oglethorpe to "the boldest hero of them all—'like death you reign, o'er silent subjects and a desert plain,'" they complained bitterly, quoting the Roman Busiris. The general had already lost his closest friend and ally, Tomochichi, whom he had buried in October 1739 among the English in Percival Square with full military honors.

Oglethorpe was to see in Georgia the betrayal of all his dreams. His greatest military triumph, his victory over the Spanish at the Battle of Bloody Marsh, which once and for all wrested British control of the colonies from the Spanish was rewarded with a court-martial. On July 5, 1742, the Spanish fleet of thirty-six sail carrying over 5000 men under the command of Don Manuel de Monteano anchored off the south end of St. Simons about a mile above Oglethorpe's works and erected a battery mounted with twenty 18-pounders. Oglethorpe destroyed his own battery, retired to his headquarters at Frederica and resorted to guerrilla war-fare, deploying his Indian allies and his Highlanders in full tartans to obstruct the approaching Spanish. His provisions at the garrison were scant and his supply lines to Savannah were successfully blocked by the Spanish fleet, facts which he managed to conceal from his little army of 700 men. On the verge of total defeat and hopelessly outnumbered, he wrought an incredible victory out of an ingenious trick. When one of his men defected to the Spanish, he dispatched him a note, imploring him to detain the enemy on the island until Oglethorpe's reinforcement of 2000 land forces and six British ships should arrive. The Spanish intercepted the note, assumed the defector was a spy, as Oglethorpe had hoped, moved immediately and while their land forces were encamped at Bloody Marsh were ambushed and all but wiped out. They "never halted until they had got under cover of the guns of their battery and ships," Hugh McCall proudly reported. Oglethorpe's reward: the Carolinians, who had refused him any military assistance, circulated pamphlets against him in Charleston and a Lieutenant Colonel William Cook, whom Oglethorpe had promoted before he went to Charleston, exhibited nineteen charges against him. In September 1743 in London, a general court-martial was ordered for his trial, to convene at the Horse Guards. A board of examiners for the court acquitted Oglethorpe, but he never returned to Georgia.

From England, he was to watch the failure of his dreams for the Indians. Mary Musgrove Bosomworth, who had been retained at 100 pounds a year to act as his interpreter to the Indians, recruit scouts and settle trading posts as lookout stations in remote places, was, despite his urgent requests, never paid. Mary and her husband, Thomas Bosomworth, the cleric who had written a scathing attack on George Whitefield's orphanage at Bethesda, led a small army of outraged Indians into Savannah to claim her title as empress and take over the land for her people. The little army was seduced by gifts of rum and trinkets, and Mary, the hauntingly beautiful princess, was thrown in jail. Eventually the Indians were given the hunting islands of Ossabaw, Sapelo and St. Catherine's, which was, a century later, to be the headquarters of the nation's first black Separatist Empire.

Even more painful to the exiled general was the introduction of slavery to the colony in 1747. Ironically, it was done in the name of Methodist evangelism. The first African slaves were brought into Hutchinson's Island to till the rice fields for Whitefield's orphanage, Bethesda. The cause seemed worthy enough. Tales abound of the religious ardor of Whitefield's orphans. One observer describes them as they were picking cotton, thrown suddenly into a wild religious fervor, dropping to their knees to confess their young sins and praying for "broken and contrite hearts." But at least one of the trustees was skeptical of so much ardor—"not a moment of innocent recreation though necessary to the health and strengthening of growing children is allowed the whole day, but much public and private prayer. . . ." And one Church of England priest observed in 1741 that many of the children "suffered. . . . in their bodies by hard useage and in their principles and manners by the mistaken Doctrine of their teachers."

When the first Negro servants were purchased for the orphan house the Reverend Mr. Boltzious charged Whitefield with "a whimsical change of sentiments, destructive to industry and morality" and summoned all the vengeance of heaven against those who were "instrumental in bringing a people under the yoke of slavery."

But Whitefield maintained it was the will of God. Wasn't it far better for the "wretched, miserable, starved" Negro fathers who were reduced to selling their own sons and daughters "to a barbarous, cruel foe to be disposed of in a Christian country where they are treated with mildness and humanity?"

After a meeting of twenty-three representatives from the colony, Hutchinson's Island was granted to Whitefield's patroness, Lady Huntingdon, who stocked it with slaves to till the rice fields to support Bethesda orphanage. Two years later, in 1749, the colony's first slave code was instituted under a cloak of benevolence. "At some time on the Lord's Day" the slaves must receive "Instruction in the Christian religion," it specified. But this was the last trustees' meeting that Oglethorpe ever attended.

Still he broods ghostlike over Savannah. His visage dominates Chippewa Square where on spring days children and their nurses mingle with peanut vendors and organ grinders, sweet sunken-faced derelicts and crisp housewives. Savannah is at the height of her beauty then when the parks are livid with blood-red azaleas, wisteria garlands the matted live oaks, and the streets are glazed with dogwood. There is a tang of roses in the air and the city, full of the heady, fevered promise of spring, reels with a giddy devil-may-care *joi de vivre*.

One never escapes the past in Savannah. Walking tours are a favorite diversion. Visitors like to explore Factors' Walk, striding past the venerable old brick buildings which headquartered the South's precarious cotton economy before the Civil War to the waterfront with its fine skein of iron bridgework and its cobblestone alleyways. Mills Lane's Spanish sailing ship, the *Cruz del Sur*, dominates the company of noisy tugs at the pier, and across the street, tucked amid the lamplit, ballast-banked little bistros, is one of the banker's most sentimental gifts to the city of his birth—the Ships of the Sea Museum which holds a replica of every ship that ever stirred a landlubber's dream.

Most of the outstanding restaurants have an authentic colonial atmosphere—the Sign of the White Hart, which has been known to send a horse-drawn carriage to pick up guests who're having a drink nearby, Tiffany House, lit by a rare collection of Tiffany lamps, and Hester's Martinique in the old City Market. But if you're from out of town, chances are you'll go first to the Pirate's House, built in 1754 as a seaman's tavern and located in the Trustees' Garden ten-acre restoration complex where the colony's original trustees first launched their ill-fated experiments in silk and wine culture in 1733. The atmosphere is studied—the walls are hung with slave auction notices and there is a heavy traffic in souvenirs—but the French crepes with seafood are authentic enough to please the most discriminating palate.

Visitors may linger on to enjoy the hospitality of the Savannah Inn and Country Club on Wilmington Island. Known familiarly as the "old Oglethorpe," the Savannah Inn was once the musty, rococo, vaguely sinister lair of the Teamsters' hierarchy, a sad, seedy palace of a hotel which had fallen into such disrepute and disrepair that "no one went there any more." But it was magnificently situated on the Wilmington River, and the pleasure boats that cruise the

Intracoastal Waterway often paused there for cocktail parties at the dock. It boasted one of the finest golf courses in the Southeast, and its banquet and meeting facilities were among the largest on the Georgia coast. It remained for an international corporation to move in with a four-million-dollar investment and the services of a crack golf architect, William Byrd of Atlanta, to make the Savannah Inn and Country Club, with one hundred fifteen guest rooms, a seventy-two par, eighteen-hole golf course and a marina, the poshest new resort on the Georgia coast.

The hotel's decor draws heavily on Savannah's past. The charming boutiques in the shopping arcade are patterned after Factors' Walk and the Peter Tondee Tavern, named for Savannah's Revolutionary tavern keeper who spent his troubled childhood at Bethesda orphanage, is decorated in the eighteenth-century idiom with copperware and enormous old rum kegs and an unforgettable view of the Wilmington River through panoramic windows. The hard-bound wine list is excellent, there is a wide selection of continental beers, and the menu includes Lobster Savannah and Chateaubriand at prices which are not unreasonable.

The tavern is one more example of Savannah's unique combination of history, aesthetics, and progress. The city fathers speak as knowledgeably of the Franciscan monks who first settled here as they do of oceanographic research, wax as eloquent about the Civil War battle of Fort Pulaski as they do about Savannah's burgeoning tourist traffic. Skipping adroitly from ocean-probing scientists to Savannah's duelists, they apologize, "You never know what century we're apt to be in." But it is this very sense of the continuity of life that gives Savannah its unique perspective. While Skidaway's leaders are guiding Savannah into a dynamic new era of research and development, the ladies of the Trustees' Garden Club are restoring the old tombstones in Colonial Cemetery. In Savannah, this is not an anachronism; it's what the city is all about.

2

Gullah

THE HAUNTED LAND

In the eerie light of flambeaux, beneath the gnarled and bearded oaks at Altama, the Gullah singers still swoop and kneel in the Buzzard Lope, a ring dance that goes back to slavery times, to the "olden days," as Bessie Jones says, "when the peoples made songs to pacify they ownself."

"Throw me anywhere in dat ole field
I don't care where you throw me, in dat ole field
Throw me over hills and mountains, in dat ole field
But still my soul is heavenbound in dat ole field . . ."

"Dey is telling the white people bout de way dey wuz buried," explains Bessie Jones, who is one of the great coastal folk singers. "Dey didn't have good caskets—dey put most anywhere in dat ole field. Dey used to call it de boneyard, where de buzzard come for he prey. But when dey heard Jesus was buried in de field of Golgotha, dey felt anywhere in dat ole field was all right. It don't matter, if you be saved."

The singers today, performing at Altama Plantation near St. Simons, can still make their audience wince, for one of the cruelest indignities of slavery was the failure of the whites to honor the ancient burial rites of the African, the ritualistic doorway to the kingdom of the blessed.

Today only the graveyards mark the mystical region of the Gullahs—a haunted land of brooding ghosts, sorcery and superstitions, intricate rituals, and a strange and lyrical language. Once it extended from Savannah to St. Mary's, cut off from the mainstream of American life by poverty, ignorance, and the splendid isolation of the pine barrens and the vast salt marsh. Here, on the great rice plantations of the nineteenth century, the customs and superstitions of half a hundred African tribes were mingled and renewed to form one of the unique cultures in the United States. It has survived the Civil War, Reconstruction, and the great world conflicts, but it is perishing now in the wake of compulsory education, affluence, and the inexorable American communications system. At Sapelo Island today, you will find TV antennae on little tin-roofed shacks papered with newsprint to divert the witches who may enter between midnight and cock crow.

The Gullahs have become teachers and preachers, lawyers and doctors; many work at the factories and military bases of Savannah and Brunswick, and if they remember the old ways, they do not practice them. But the Gullah culture persists in the little fishing villages of Valona, Bellview, and the dead town of Sunbury, a ghostly strip of ridgeland where once stood the port that rivaled Savannah. The unpainted houses, with their windows rimmed in blue to ward off haunts, their sandy dooryards scratched by frizzled chickens searching for conjure bags, are all the white man usually sees of the Gullah culture. That and the little graveyards, guarded by primitive wooden heads of animals and men, glinting blindly through glass eyes. The graves bear mute testimony to the dead. Here lies the broken crockery they used—the white ironstone plates, the coffee mugs, the pitchers and rusting porcelain washbowls. There are alarm clocks to wake the dead on judgment day, kerosene lamps to light the way along the dark and unknown path of eternity, and sometimes the last objects that were used—a roll of toilet paper on one; on another empty bottles of cough syrup, Bayer aspirin and Vick's VapoRub and, beside a little rough-hewn wooden marker, an empty whiskey bottle.

Some historians believe the word Gullah derives from the Golla tribe of Liberia, and perhaps it does. But early newspaper advertisements indicate that the first coastal slaves came from the Gambia and Niger River sections of Africa. Later, the Gold Coast, from the Congo to the southern end of Portuguese West Africa, was the base of operations, but many slaves were captured in the villages of the interior and driven to the coast in long, death-ridden marches. The *Wanderer* brought the last, illegal cargo of slaves to Jekyll Island in 1858, and there was at least one Gullah, Uncle Robert, of Wilmington Island, who remembered hearing stories about them.

"When one of those Africans die, it wuz bery sad," he told an interviewer from the University of Georgia years ago.

"When a man's countryman die, he set right wid 'em all night. Den in de mawnin he go out and pray to de sun. Dem Africans ain't got no Christianity. Dey ain hab no regulah religion. Dey jes pray to the sun and moon and sometime to a big star. After they pray, they come in and put deah han on deah frien and say good-by. Den dey go back home."

Isolated on the vast rice plantations of the coast, with their white masters in residence only a short part of the year, the coastal Negroes evolved a unique language—haunting, poetic, and to most whites, almost totally incomprehensible. Historians, the same who attribute dances like the Buzzard Lope to the influence of the English ring dances, have tried to trace the Gullah speech to the seventeenth- and eighteenth-century British dialects. Actually, it is a combination of English, African, and the most elemental and lyrical onomatopoeia.

The majestic blue heron who sweeps and dives across the emerald marshes at Sapelo is called "poor Joe"—Padzo is the name of a similar heron in Africa. The tortoise is called a cooter; near Timbuktu, it is called a kuta. And the small wild horses that roam the coastal islands are known as takis, the West African name for horse. You'll hear them speak of "toting" cotton, a word that derives from tota, in Congo "to pick up." And the Foulah numerals to ten are still in use.

The old plantation books from Kelvin Grove on St. Simons abound with names still common on the coast—Bina (Tuesday), Cuffy (Friday), quanimina (Wednesday). The custom of naming children for the day of their birth derives from the Eve tribes of Dahomey and Tago, who borrowed the custom from the Twai people.

Linguists who have studied the Gullah speech point out that the noun usually has the same form in the plural as in the singular; the Gullah words for time are tenuous and vague, the subject is placed before the verb in interrogative sentences and the word order is similar to the West African. "Dem bit em," the Gullah will tell you, meaning, "He was beaten," or "De God wok," meaning, "It is God's work."

If there were a dictionary of Gullah, it would sing with onomatopoeia:

Bidi bidi—a small bird

Bim—violently

Hu hu—owl

Pak, pak, pak—to knock

Ban, ban, ban—to pound

A refrain of pure African distinguishes most Gullah songs. "New Rice and Okra, Na Na; Eat Some and Leave Some, Na, Na," they sing, meaning "I'll Come, I'll Come." And you can hear Gullah children singing African chants at the Saturday night oyster roasts at the Church of God on St. Simons Island.

But on Sunday mornings, at the Harlem Road Church of God, when Bessie Jones jangles the tambourine and the congregation thumps tin washboards, they are more apt to be singing their own response to twentieth-century Christian atheism.

> God's Not Dead
> He Sure Is Not
> Jesus Is Alive
> Oh God's Not Dead . . .

The Gullahs, introduced to Christianity in the early nineteenth century by plantation missionaries like Dr. C. C.

Jones of Midway, are devoutly religious. To the rigid Presbyterian and Congregationalist rituals of their masters, they added elements of pure joy—the holy laugh, a rich staccato "ha ha!" the holy kiss—the warm, open-hearted embrace with which they conclude their ceremonies; and the holy dances—the elemental rhythms which they do in a trance-like state to the ringing of drums and tambourines:

> We got to move when the spirit say move
> Shout when the spirit say shout
> We got to sing when the spirit say sing
> Thank God for to be converted. Halle-lu-jah!

Since the early days of the praise houses, they have been a Christ-haunted people. Yet in their African heritage there was nothing analogous to the Christ concept of the God-connected man, except possibly the Ebo's female deity, Eka Ghassi, mother of the all-powerful thunder God. Traditionally, of course, they were polytheistic. Some tribes like the Eve had a reverence for the plant or animal from which his clan took its name, and sun worship was common. The older Negroes at White Bluff can remember their grandparents on St. Catherine's Island praying at the rising and setting of the sun, with a reverent refrain, "meena, mina, mo," which the plantation children adopted as a counting game. Their religion was not allied with moral ideas. Sin was an insult to the Gods or neglect of the Gods, that vast company of captious and capricious spirits who peopled both this world and the next. Instinctively they accepted the fact that they were their brother's keeper. "Death begins by one person," was an old Bantu proverb, a saying which at least one McIntosh County preacher recalls when he warns his congregation: "If a man digs a pit for his neighbor, he digs one for himself." African proverbs are often heard on the coast. "When you eat with the devil, you must have a long fork," the Gullahs say, echoing a proverb from Dutch Guinea. And, "never forget the bridge that carries you over."

The older Gullahs, with their mystical other-worldliness, are still essentially polytheistic. They believe the spirits of the departed make frequent visits to earth, and those who are "born with the caul," a hypersensitivity to the occult, can see and talk with them. Ghosts abound, as in West Africa, where every man can expect to meet his "duppy" at least once in his lifetime. And in the little settlements like Sandfly, some still talk of being ridden by witches at night, an ancient belief of the Vais.

According to the Vais legend, when a witch comes in the door he takes off his skin and lays it aside in the house, rides the victim through the night and returns him to his bed in the morning. "Dey jes sit on your chest and ride you," Uncle Robert told the University of Georgia researchers. "You wake up and feel lak you smudderhin. If you kin get duh succulation and tro um off, it all right."

In Savannah, the Geechee Negroes, who take their name from their birthplace near the Ogeechee River, follow the old Vais custom of sprinkling salt and pepper in the corners of the room, a practice which is supposed to prevent the witch from putting on her skin. At Harris Neck, the Gullahs put a broom across their front doors to keep the witches out, and on Sapelo those who are tormented by hags put a knife or a Bible under their pillows.

Through generations of oppression, the Gullahs have learned to appease the spirits, both good and evil, with hundreds of strange little rituals, practiced so long and so un-questioningly that only the very old can tell you their mystical derivations. At Darien, the Gullahs never sweep out trash after dark. The young people will tell you that to do so is to sweep your luck away. But the old know it is to sweep out the spirits of the departed. If it must be done, one can remedy the evil by throwing out a live coal or simply repeating, "Move on Friend."

To the Gullah, the hoot of the owl or the plaintive cry of the whippoorwill still presages death, an ancient Vais belief. To ward off its evil, he turns his pockets inside out, his shoes upside down, or sticks a shovel into the live coals of a fire. And when he sneezes, he will, in the ritual of the Bakongo tribesman, wave his hand and say "Far from you," as if warding off an evil spirit.

Superstitions are endless, and few white people ignore them. It is, the Gullah will tell you, bad luck to get your first look at the new moon through the trees. For good luck, the moon must be glimpsed over a clearing, preferably over the salt marsh or the ocean. They often wear red to appease the evil spirits, recalling, perhaps, that it was the great red cloths, hung on the masts of slaving ships, which duped some of their unwary ancestors into slavery. Evil spirits hate iron, they say; they hang iron horsehoes over their doorways, and use only iron needles, never steel pins, to remove splinters.

The Gullahs believe that wood that has been struck by lightning is unlucky; before they touch it, they sprinkle it with dishwater to break the spell. When they wash a teacup, they set it upside down on the drainboard so the bad luck will run out. And if you ask them how they feel, they will

1. Alan Walker of Sapelo

2. *(left)* The old Reynolds estate on Sapelo

3. *(above)* Gullah cemetery on Sapelo

4. On the beach at Sapelo

answer "fair," or "so so." To appear too healthy or happy might provoke the evil spirits.

Visitors are never allowed to put their hats on the bed—this brings bad luck to the house—and they must always go out the same door by which they entered. Painting the front door blue brings good fortune to the family. One can protect a home against fire by keeping a tortoise-shell cat, and a smutty-nosed cat always brings luck. But a kitten who comes to the door after dark brings trouble unless you can make it stay by rubbing butter on its paws.

The island fishermen, who depend on the coastal waters for their meager living, have evolved their own obeisance to the gods. They spit on their bait for luck, throw away the thirteenth shrimp or fiddler crab, and always start out with the same rig they used for the last big catch. If anyone wishes them good luck, their luck is sure to be bad. A flight of pelicans or gulls is a good omen, but only if there's an uneven number. They will keep any small oddly shaped piece of driftwood as a good luck charm, and they hang horseshoe crabs over the front door, the points down, so their good fortune won't run out. If a night bird, harbinger of evil, flies in front of them on the beach, they make the sign of the cross on the sand—a symbol which they use frequently. On St. Simons, children are sometimes protected against troubling spirits by a cross, etched in ashes on their forehead in the ancient Anglican tradition of Ash Wednesday.

The coastal whites seldom question these customs, for they have learned that the Gullahs are in some ways much closer to reality than they are. Miss Bessie Lewis, the gentle, white-haired historian of Pine Harbor, remembers all too well the death of her yardman, Alexander. Peering into his morning tea, he saw a "side of beef," a sure sign of death, and canceled the trip he'd planned to Darien that day. But before dusk he had met his death in a freak drowning accident.

The Gullahs tend to view adversity not as the workings of fate but as the revenge of a personal enemy brought about by the mystic workings of the conjure doctor. They do not talk of "bad luck," but of "bad mouth," set against them by the enemy, and they view the world with the primitive paranoia of the Bakongo tribes, who believed all sickness was the result of witchcraft. "There ain't supposed to be any such thing as nachel death here," says Lizzie Jenkins of the settlement of Sandfly. "Everything that happens is caused by conjure. They just don't leave anything to God."

Sorcery is widely practiced by modern root doctors who range from Uncle John Bowen of St. Catherine's Island—"a man of so much devilment he finally eat heself and die"—to Ophelia Baker, "Madam Truth," a Sandfly fortuneteller and clairvoyant who, body jerking, eyes rolling spasmodically, advises on business and love affairs, predicts the future, and has, she vows, a remedy for "every trouble, for a spirit have brung it on me." On Wilmington Island, stories abound about Smart McCall, who once managed to free a local Negro from a murder charge. According to Uncle Robert, on the day of the trial a buzzard—conjured up by McCall—flew into the courthouse window and circled the judge's bench so menacingly that he abruptly dismissed the case.

While African root doctors use bitter-tasting grasses, herbs, and barks, the coastal doctors tend to use charms made of nail parings, bits of hair, and graveyard dust. At Sandfly, they will tell you that "dust from tracks" makes a powerful charm. Some charms are sold commercially—Adam and Eve

Root, Lucky Majo Drops, Black Cat Ashes and Courting Powder. Burrs Butler of Grimball's Point on the languidly beautiful Isle of Hope, uses the bone of a black cat to ward off conjure and cure sickness. Like most Gullahs, he wears a dime tied to his ankle with a string; if it grows dark or tarnished, he knows he has been conjured.

"Witches and root men is the same thing. They can turn themselves into any shape—a insect, a cat and a dog and any kind of animal. They can go through any kind of hole to get at you," says Shrimp Hall, of White Bluff, echoing a Nigerian belief that witches and wizards have animal counterparts and can assume the form of owls, lizards, vultures, and night birds.

Tales of conjure abound on the coast. Mary Hunter of Savannah will tell you how she was conjured by the woman who later ran off with her husband. "I came home, stepped in a hole by the door and deah was a bottle fix with some things in it. Right then and there I took such a misery in my left side and then I swell up all over. My hands was twice their size. I sprinkle black pepper and potash in de hole where de bottle was and it bile up. Then some friends wash me off in whiskey every day and soon I was all right. But when de twins was born, the boy twin have a lil hole right in the left side where I have the misery from the fixing. He live nine days before he die."

The chicken is a mystical figure in Gullah lore. White chickens are still sacrificed at some funerals, and though modern breeding techniques have made the frizzled chicken a rarity, they are occasionally seen in Gullah dooryards scratching for conjure bags that may be hidden beneath the doorstep by an enemy. A frizzled chicken, Miss Bessie Lewis explains, is a genetic accident that looks "like he was pulled through a knot hole—backwards and wet." If the chicken loses his feathers, his owner can be sure he has scratched up a conjure bag.

No man is a match for conjure, and when the master of conjure, the root doctor, tangles with his archenemy, the medical doctor, the results are usually tragic. Old timers at White Bluff can tell you how Smart McCall put such a powerful spell on Dr. Rogers' horse that he drove the kindly physician into a tree and killed him.

Despite the root doctor's reputation for invulnerability, physicians like Dr. William Tailer of Darien have a wide practice among the Negroes who man the shrimp boats and work in the turpentine forests of McIntosh County. His patients never have an ache or pain, they suffer from "miseries." They often complain of "cascading" (vomiting), and the "blind staggers," a reaction from high blood pressure which afflicts many of the coastal Negroes. He sees little actual hunger among the Gullahs, but he has seen a tragic number of needless deaths among Gullah children whose parents tend to wait for "school shots" to immunize their young.

Dr. Tailer is still baffled by some of their cures—wearing green leaves or match sticks in their hair, or tying their hair up in braids to ease a "dropped palate" (sore throat). They have come to him with fever bush leaves on a broken ankle, with cobwebs, sugar, and sometimes dirt packed into an open wound, with wads of salt plastered on their heads to ease a headache or a fever. Most of them wear an asafetida bag, like a St. Christopher, around their necks. This evil-smelling root, used in the days before belladonna, is worn, he says to ward off colds, though some of his patients swear it keeps away evil spirits.

Like many whites, Dr. Tailer has become a collector of Gullah parables, jotting them down on scraps of paper between patients. A Gullah literature does not exist, outside of a few prayers, two or three accounts of hurricanes, and the ring dances and songs compiled by Mrs. Lydia Parrish. But a definitive study of Negro mythology was done by Charles C. Jones, son of the Midway missionary who preached to the slaves on the rice plantations of Liberty County. Coastal children know these stories by heart and can repeat them in the dialect which Jones mastered with remarkable fidelity, long before dialect stories became the province of the southern "moonlight and magnolia school." "Bur Squirle bin berry busy du gedder hickry nut on de groun fuh feed heself and he fambly der winter time . . ." he would begin a story, long before the Uncle Remus tales were penned, and he accompanied his delicious tales of animal one-upmanship with a unique glossary of Gullah words.

But there are two Gullah folk tales seldom shared with white people—the tale of the self-propelled hoe, which derives from an old Housa legend, and the tale of the flying Africans, a half-formed myth born out of the wrenching oppression of slavery.

"Lots of slaves wuz brought over from Africa could fly. Dere folks can fly even now," Uncle Jack, of Wilmington Island used to say, and Burris Butler, of Grimball's Point, adds, "Dey tell me dem people could do all kine uh curous things. They could make farm tools work for them jes by talking tuh em. And some of them could disappear at will. Wist! And dey'd be gone." And there is a wizened, white-haired old Gullah, nodding on his porch in the shade of a crepe myrtle bush, who claims his uncle had the power to fly. "Ef dey believe in this magic, they could escape and fly back to Africa," he says.

Old Shrimp Hall, who was born a slave of Jacob Waldberg on St. Catherine's Island, remembers stories his mother told him of a man and wife who could "work conjure and fly."

"Any time dey want to dey would fly back to Africa and den come back again to de plantation. Dey come back cuz dey have some chillun who didn hab de power to fly and hab to stay on the plantation."

Prince Sneed, of White Bluff heard a similar story from his grandmother, who was also a slave on St. Catherine's. "Ole man Waldburg own some slaves wut wuzn climatize," says Mr. Sneed. "An he wuk them hard and one day they wuz hoein de fields and de driver come over and two of um was under a tree in the shade and de hoe was working by emself. De driver say, whut diz? and dey say 'Kum Buuba Yali, Jum Bumba Tambe, Kum Kunka Yali, Kum Kuma Tambe' quick like. Den dey rize off duh ground and fly back to Africa. Nobody ever see em no mo. Muh gran see dat wid her own eyes."

While few slaves had the power to fly, death offered a final release to all of them, and on some plantations births were mourned, while death was celebrated with joyous rituals that included a nightlong wake called a "setting-up," ring dances, animal sacrifices, and fasting. The drums announced each death and funeral. "Boom, boom, boom, dey went," recalls Uncle Robert. "Dey'd go on and on. We called it de death march."

Most Gullahs still hold the ancient Ebo belief that only the proper observance of the funeral ceremony allows the soul to go to God and its final destination. Otherwise it becomes a wanderer on earth, haunting houses and burial grounds. They also believe the spirit of the deceased knows all that is going on and is sensitive to the quality of the mourning and the details of the funeral.

The death watch, which originated in Dahomey, is still a vital part of the Gullah funeral ceremony. At the "setting up," food is set out for the dead and coffee and white bread are served to the mourners, who sit in a circle around the body, sobbing and keening—an elemental, rhythmic, profoundly sad humming which is the refrain of every Gullah funeral. When Ophelia Baker conducts a funeral at Sandfly, she instructs the mourners to pour coffee on the ground for the deceased, following an ancient Dahomey ritual in which the akovi, or guard, anoints the corpse with three morsels of bread and three drops of water.

The custom of putting the effects of the dead on the grave also goes back to Dahomey, where a small house was built upon the beach to hold the valuables of the dead—the statues, clocks, vases, and porcelains which were treasured in life. Three other tribes, the Benga, the Mponque, and the Fang, carried boxes of the dead man's goods—clothes, hardware, and crockery—to be laid beside the body, which in those days was covered with leaves and branches. In West Africa, food, tobacco, and rum were placed on the graves, and Zulu widows always broke pottery over the graves of their husbands. Today, the broken pottery on Gullah graves is said to symbolize the brokenness of life. But some Gullahs will tell you it is simply to prevent these valuables from being stolen. Many of these graves are also marked by charm roots similar to the ones which Stanley's pioneer officers found on Congo graves during the nineteenth century.

The Sudanese custom of slaughtering animals is still observed at some Gullah funerals. Usually a white chicken or a hog is slaughtered, but occasionally a hound dog is killed and left on the barbed wire fence to bleed on the crockery covered graves at the Sunbury cemetery.

Many Gullahs still observe the second funeral, a deeply religious All Saints' Day which derives from the Ebo conviction that no human soul can attain to the peaceful habitations of his ancestors without a second funeral. These Gullahs believe in a primitive purgatory, a region of the dead in which the soul exists like a beast on grass and leaves until, with the second funeral, he is ushered into his ancestors' abode in the world of the spirits.

The Gullahs, as Cruickshank wrote of the Gold Coast Africans, "are unanimous in thinking that there is in man a spirit which survives the body; that it is conscious of what is going on on earth and has some power, some influence over their destiny."

To the Gullahs, the ultimate tragedy is not death, but the meager and impoverished funeral which deprives the dead of his triumphal entry into paradise. At Pinpoint, a little settlement of tin-roofed shacks huddled beneath the majestic live oaks on the black-silk mud flats of the Savannah River, the Gullahs are still haunted by the tragedy of Catherine DeLancy, who was murdered by her husband, Bo-Cat, on a Friday the thirteenth in February 1932. Bo-Cat took her out to Raccoon Key in a weathered bateau, struck her with an oar and set her adrift in the ebb tide at Hell's Gate, where her body was washed ashore and ravaged by buzzards. In the evenings, when the oysters and fiddler crabs "click, clack" monotonously beneath the weathered docks, they sing a song of Catherine that goes like this:

> He put her in the boat
> They began to float
> It's a shame how Bo-Cat done his wife.
>
> He knock her in de brest
> And duh oah done duh res
> It's a shame how Bo-Cat done his wife.

The real tragedy was that there could be no setting-up for Catherine DeLancy, no death watch, no coffee and bread to sustain her on her journey into eternity. One hundred people rose to testify at her funeral at the Sweet Field of Eden Church. "Catherine DeLancy was a sister of the Lord," "She wuz a chile of Jesus" . . . "She walk in the way of righteousness," they vowed, while their keening evoked all the infinite sorrow of life. They heaped the powdery gray sand of Pinpoint on her grave, then covered it with the things she had treasured in life—a lamp chimney, a perfume bottle, a blue and white china pitcher. "But the spirit has never res in dat grave," they'll tell you today at Pinpoint. Catherine DeLancy still weeps among the marsh grasses at Hell's Gate, one of the many restless spirits who haunt the mystical country of the coastal Gullahs.

3

Hilton Head

THE LAST BASTION

In a casually elegant drawing room at Hilton Head, a middle-aged chain-store executive switched off the 7 P.M. television news, drained his martini, and declared bitterly, "The only answer is to find yourself a bastion." Harvard was under siege by a vanguard of black militants, and doting, mannerly old Charleston, torn by a hospital workers' strike, was an armed camp. But his balcony overlooked the moss-shrouded oaks and the moon-drenched beach of Hilton Head.

Increasingly, the men with the means are finding their bastion against national turbulence behind the sentineled gates of Hilton Head Island, just thirty miles north of Savannah. Ironically, this storied island, as the headquarters of some 13,000 Federal troops during the Civil War, was the birthplace of the Port Royal Experiment, one of the great, bold, visionary offensives of American Puritanism, designed to deliver the newly unshackled slaves of Hilton Head and its neighboring islands into the promised land of New England liberalism. Here a peace corps of Harvard and Andover graduates, Unitarian missionaries, noted abolitionists, and Yankee schoolmarms forged the philosophies of separatism, "heart power," reparations and land redistribution which made Hilton Head a national showcase of radical reconstruction, philosophies which, lost in that forgotten era of history, have returned, like unlaid ghosts, to haunt the more conservative of the affluent couples who talk darkly of chaos and anarchy over fruited gin drinks around the kidney shaped pool at the William Hilton Inn.

From the Palmetto Bay Marina which attracts most of the lavish pleasure crafts that cruise the inland waterway, they can see the lovely beaches and ominous pine barrens of Daufuskie Island—one of the last enclaves of Gullah culture, where 125 Negroes live out their lives in privy-less shanties, drawing water from poisonously contaminated wells. The failure of the Port Royal Experiment left a tragic legacy of hunger, isolation, and disease. Seventy-three per cent of the children of Beaufort County are reported to have worms and, Sea Pines, the reigning colony on Hilton Head, has launched its own war against parasites.

Sensitive to the specter of hunger in the surrounding lowlands, the officials of Hilton Head deny theirs is a millionaires' retreat. But in its short and sensationally successful history as a resort, it has managed to attract a higher percentage of Who's Who listees than any township in the United States. The new aristocracy of achievers—artists and statesmen, corporate executives and writers—has found within its closely screened confines a scrupulously planned and rigidly controlled last refuge of the good life. Here are preserved the vanishing sureties—familiar faces at the Plantation Club, a pervasive sense of history and a meticulously ordered environment where the fierce, shattering, and liberating elements of the coastal wilderness have been discreetly curbed—the terrain has been sculpted into nine superb and scenic golf courses by architects like George Cobb and Robert Trent Jones; alligators laze in lagoons between the new condominiums at Sea Pines Plantation, and wildlife—the opossums and turkeys, the deer and bobcat—are relegated to a two-mile conservation park.

The Hilton Head landscape so seduced Hinesville lumberman Fred Hack that he abandoned his plans for timbering the island to develop it into one of the most prestigious spas on the Carolina coast. It was a young associate, Charles Fraser, a "Liberty County boy" he calls himself, a graduate of Yale Law School with a genius for visionary speculation, who created Sea Pines Plantation, the pioneer community on Hilton Head. In the fifties, his dedication to aesthetics, to retaining the integrity of the landscape at the cost of all the crasser elements of commerce—neon signs, billboards, and haphazard, high-density building—was a bold and perilous innovation in development that most hardheaded businessmen considered foolhardy. A Japanese landscape architect, Sasaki, with an oriental reverence for the land, has created at Sea Pines a leisure community where discreetly elegant homes mesh with the landscape of dunes and glades; the live oak forests and secluded beaches have been left intact, and the grounds of the inns, the villas, and the exclusive Plantation

[61]

Club are ablaze with azaleas and studded with jewel-like lagoons. Since the bridge opened in 1956, Sea Pines has become one of the nation's outstanding planned communities, a venture so spectacularly successful that it has set the tone for every new spa on the Southern coast, from the posh Sea Palms golf colony at St. Simons to Fripp Island, out of Beaufort, dominated by a golf course noted for its ingenious water hazards and ringed by a splendid beach once visited by British privateers. The new breed of developers have become voracious predators of the coastal wilderness and Charles Fraser, who was known in the fifties as "the Golden Boy of the Golden Isles" has matured to hear his daring concept of the aesthetic development rapped by purists as "cosmetics for rape." Success threatens even his own bastion at Sea Pines. The Heritage Classic at Jack Nicklaus' new Harbour Course is beginning to rival the Augusta National and the land beyond Sea Pines is being slashed into canals for a novel waterfront spa called Palmetto Dunes.

Already a popular but friendly rival is Fred Hack's Port Royal Plantation—a colony of fine homes, golf courses, a luxurious clubhouse and a seventy-four-unit motel located near the headland first sighted by the Indian slave trader Pedro de Quexos on August 18, 1521, a discovery which was to usher in the spiritual tyranny of Spanish Catholicism among the Indians. A hundred years later it was christened Hilton Head by Captain William Hilton, who claimed it for England and returned to Carlisle Bay in January 1664 to report on the rich yield of fish and game, wild fruit and fowl. "The ayr is clear and sweet, the country very pleasant and delightful. And we would wish that all they that want a happy settlement of our English nation were well transported here."

Rare birds nurtured in two rookeries and the arboretum of hundreds of indigenous trees and plants bespeak Hack's feeling for the landscape—a gut feeling which may derive from the fact that he is descended from a pirate cartographer, William Hack, who drew up a manuscript map of Carolina in 1664. The landscape is preserved not only by his sense of aesthetics but by some tight regulations—the strict prohibition of condominiums or any multi-unit rental housing projects, the secreting of utility lines underground, a strict architectural approval board and the fact that the cost of homes ranges from $50,000 to $100,000.

Port Royal's overwhelming sense of history pervades even the two superb golf courses—the eighteen-hole Barony and the nine-hole Robber's Row carved out of the dunes and forests by golf architect George Cobb. At the Barony, the golfer tees off from the top of the breastworks of Fort Sherman, built in 1861 after the Confederate Fort Walker was overrun by Federal Marines in a massive amphibious invasion. The deeply forested par three, hole six, borders Bayley's Barony, a 1698 land grant which was confiscated after the Revolution by the new government under George Washington. And at Robber's Row course, walking down the number three fairway, the golfer treads the ghostly main street of what was once a burgeoning city of some 50,000 Federal troops, who converged at the vortex of the coastal blockade to prey on the feeble Confederate Navy.

This was the headquarters of the Port Royal Experiment, launched by the New York National Freedmen's Association to bring the northern primer and the New England virtues to some 10,000 slaves who had been abandoned when their masters fled the region after Fort Walker was overrun by Federal Marines. Quite specifically, the young peace corps missionaries of the Experiment—"Gideonites" they called themselves—were to teach the "contraband" Negroes "civilization and Christianity . . . order, industry, economy and self reliance and to elevate them in the scale of humanity by inspiring them with self respect." Their leader, Boston attorney Edward Pierce, declared they were the "choicest young men of New England—some of whom the world was scarce worthy." Another observer, listening to their impassioned hymns on the deck of the steamer *Atlantis*, noted their beards and mustaches, their eccentricities of dress and said, "You would have doubted whether it was the adjournment of a John Brown meeting or the tag end of a broken down phalanstery." Certainly it was in the spirit of John Brown that they came, these zealous, questing innocents, so tortured by the unholy evils of slavery that its "weird spirit" seemed to oppress even the haunting beauty of the coastal landscape. As the *Atlantis* neared Hilton Head, Austa French, wife of Mansfield French, the chaplain they called the "White Jesus," confided to her diary: "There steals over you the feeling that you are passing under a great cloud of accumulated wrongs, in which you seem mysteriously implicated, the vague feeling that you have done something awful somewhere in the dim past . . . Slavery is written upon the shore, the trees, the sky, the air . . . the enormous black hawks with their screams seem to be its very spirit. No wonder they 'caw, caw, caw' over this land—mean vultures, waiting for blood."

According to Edward Pierce, the sea island Negroes had become an "abject race, . . . more docile and submissive than those of any locality." Their deliverers embraced them with cries of "Sisters and brothers, you are free!" and then, ignorant of the simplest rudiments of agriculture, imposed on them the old tyranny of cotton. In his burning zeal to free the Negro from his shackles, Chaplain French accompanied Federal gunboats on foraging raids along the Georgia coast. "Abolitionist thieves," a Belleville plantation mistress called these parties of "black Yankees" who, led by Chaplain French, surrounded her home and freed fifty-eight slaves, forcing them off the plantation at gun point. In a letter to her three sons who were fighting with the Confederacy, she described the impassioned chaplain, who had assumed "the livery of the court of heaven to serve the devil," described him as he strode up the steps of her home, proclaiming that "the skirt of my garment will never be stained with the blood of slaves" and then, turning to the bewildered slaves, announced "we have come to clothe, to educate, to free these poor people, to teach them the Bible and prepare them for heaven."

The Port Royal Negroes, those who had been left behind by their masters and those who were forcibly delivered to this promised land, referred to the "Gideonites" regime as the "time of confusion." "We don't know who we be," they complained to Laura Towne, schoolmarm at Frogmore, as their spiritual liberators drove them from their little vegetable gardens out into the cotton fields, introduced them to a baffling wage system and dismissed the blazing truth of the divinity of Christ with dreary Unitarian sermons on thrift, virtue, and industry.

Chaplain French alone understood the power of evangelical religion, reporting to Secretary Chase that "the Unitarians don't get hold of things in the right way, for the people are mostly Baptist and like emotional religion better than rational." But the "Gideonites" never grasped the mysticism and passion of the Gullah's faith. They were shocked by the primitive, orgiastic, ecstatic celebrations of the Divine in the little plantation praise houses. The shouts—"day oh, day oh," —the holy kisses, the holy dances, the frenetic, trance-like African processionals around the altar seemed barbarous to them. Their stern logic was baffled by the Gullah's faith in the miracle of the Resurrection, a phenomenon scarcely mirac-ulous to a people who understood all too well the presence of death in life, who saw with a mystic's vision the ghosts who dwelled among them. For all their New England virtues, they had never understood the African's awe of evil—his faith in the terrible power of conjure. They cursed the Gul-lah's slowness, failing to understand his unique sense of time, his sense of dwelling in eternity. They berated the super-stitions that reflected his reverence for life—the evil of the black cat, the good fortune of the shell of a horseshoe crab hung over the front door. Nor did they grasp the Gullah's feeling for the land, his dialogue with nature, with the shift-ing tides, the ghostly forests, the undulating marshes.

But they did, in haylofts and barns and praise houses, in-troduce the Negro to the northern primer, a magic talisman to a people who had been forbidden to learn to write by the slave code of 1740, forbidden to learn to read by an 1834 law designed to protect them from the liberating message of abolitionist literature. In the infinite promise of the ABC's, the "contrabands" finally grasped the magnificent vision of freedom, only to see it shattered when, under orders from Major General David Hunter of the Department of the South, they were forcibly conscripted into military service, driven from their plantation homes, torn from the arms of their hysterical wives, given a plug of tobacco and a half-dollar and herded off to Hilton Head where, their former masters had warned them, they would be deported to Cuba and sold back into slavery. They were then technically free men, laboring under the assurances of the "Gideonites" who promised them not only their freedom but massive reparations, the sum total of society's debt to them for the accumulated wrongs of slavery.

The promises of the "Gideonites"—all the golden promises of freedom—were inevitably betrayed by human folly, by the greed of northern speculators, the bureaucratic machinations of Republican politicians, and the violent racism of the Federal troops. Those "contrabands" who were not forced into the "Gospel Army" were conscripted into forced labor at Savannah's Fort Pulaski. Their promised lands, the lands set aside for "heads of families of the African race," were sold to northern speculators and they were terrorized by the Federal troops who stole their livestock and attacked their women "like marauders in an enemy's territory," wrote Laura Towne of the atrocities at Frogmore on St. Helena's Island. In their elemental disillusionment, the blacks agreed with her cook Rina that "we just wish all the white folks would go away and let us live by ourselves," a sentiment that was to lead to the nation's first experiment in Black Separatism, a strange and tenuous empire headquartered at St. Catherine's Island below Savannah. And the "Gideonites," as they wended their way north after the war, could only conclude bitterly that "revolutions can go backwards."

Today all that remains of the Port Royal Experiment is the Penn Community Center at Frogmore, near Hilton

Head, an outgrowth of Laura Towne's little school, which is now a training center for community action. It was a spiritual refuge for Dr. Martin Luther King, who came here to rest and to write between his agonized assaults on the American conscience. Today, poor blacks from remote little hamlets throughout the South make pilgrimages to the center to be instructed in the heady new techniques of confrontation by dedicated young liberals—many of them student volunteers—the spiritual heirs of the "Gideonites."

Acutely sensitive to the "weird spirit" which still hovers over this land, an SCLC leader from Charleston, speaking in one of the ascetic meeting halls, may harp on the symbolic fact that the slave block is a Charleston tourist attraction and that the blacks are still laboring under that ancient legacy. There is talk of violent upheavals, of the "criminal values of America," of the betrayal of the Bill of Rights. "We're going to sock it to America with yellows, blacks and whites—we're going to point the way for the rest of the world," the militants proclaim, echoing the Port Royal leaders who once threatened, when the blacks were in jeopardy of losing their promised lands, "If unchaining the fiend will work our deliverance, then let the fiend be unchained."

The new militancy has finally penetrated the long, mute despair of the lyrical, hag-ridden, Christ-haunted Gullahs of the low country. The young volunteers at Penn have guided them through the bureaucratic labyrinth of welfare rights, food stamps, Medicare and the OEO, and have nurtured at last an indigenous leadership, a Negro matriarchy of indomitable, impassioned and aggrieved earth mothers. Women like Hazel Fraser, of the Welfare Rights Organization, a gargantuan, infinitely wise mother of ten children, housed in a proud, unpainted shanty, are speaking their piece, and speaking it so compellingly that hunger has finally become the first order of American business. The fine yeast of hope is fermenting in the black-silk mud of the marsh flats; a change, a promise is in the sea-stung air for the first time since the Hilton Head slaves, done out of their promised land by their Yankee deliverers, realized that freedom was a snare and a delusion, a doorway from the tyranny of the driver's lash to the far more complicated, inexplicable and thus less tolerable slavery of carpetbag capitalism.

The new breed of "Gideonites" are, for the most part, affluent youngsters, satiated with the carbonated lies of the Pepsi generation, who have come to the South Carolina coast to immerse themselves in the enduring truths of human suffering. Scorning the old myths of Christendom, they have sampled even the most spurious fruits of the spirit—astrology, the prophecies of Edgar Cayce, the occultism of Bishop Pike—searching for another dimension, a new forefront of mystery. They have found it in men like Tecumseh Capers, the Black-Indian son of a coastal root doctor who is recognized among the young as the high priest of Gullah mysticism.

A lean, lithe man with the Indian's strong, planed features and the passionate eyes of a visionary, Capers lives the contemplative life at Frogmore in a lean-to asserted by a towering heap of bleached white bones from which he fashions his strange and incredibly beautiful jewelry. He barbers two days a week; a black iron, curlicued barber's chair dominates his workroom like a throne. On the walls hang a painting of the Last Supper, a display of African hair styles—the dandyism of the new cult of Black Beauty—and a collection, mounted on black velvet, of his subtly colored necklaces and earrings of bones. A raccoon scratches and gnaws through stacks of old newspapers and a table is heaped with pomades and cologne, bones and chisels. Only a few visitors are shown his finest craft—the rare shells painted with Madonnas and heads of Christ, icons of Gullah mysticism.

Occasionally he will reveal to one of the Penn volunteers the light of that other world which is his peculiar province, leading them down the Frogmore Road to the Chapel of Ease, a tabby ruin of a church where planters like John Fripp worshiped before the Civil War and left on the moss-grown tombstones the poetry of their ancient griefs—"I miss you so my Ludi, I miss you every day." Here, the young students will tell you, in the graveyard beneath the bearded oaks, a ghostly light appears, illumines the tombstones and gilds the shrouds of moss. With a word from Tecumseh the light turns red and blazes with such a terrible, crimson ferocity that Tecumseh himself becomes incandescent. The light is said to be the tortured spirit of a slave who was beheaded by his master, an eternal indictment of the men who once assuaged their guilt with the bread and wine of the Eucharist at the Chapel of Ease on St. Helena's Island.

Mystery is still the special province of the sea islands. At Hilton Head, it is threatened by the bulldozers, which are taming the land into a playground, and by the insulation of affluence, of muted lounges where only the old Brady Civil War photographs suggest the spiritual battles that were fought here. But those who leave the beaten track of the golf courses, scenic drives and busy marinas can still discover old Indian artifacts in fields once tilled by the island slaves. On the marshes' edge, they may stumble on a Gullah cemetery, the graves marked by faded pink wreaths of plastic gladioli, empty bottles of Mylanta and rubbing alcohol—the last frail hope of the dead—and rough cement crosses inscribed with a labored scrawl—"Asleep in Jesus; oh how sweet." They will find that ghosts still haunt this island—visitors have heard carriage bells and whoops of laughter on an abandoned path once driven by the coastal planters. And a dialogue with nature is still possible; there are sudden, surprising encounters—flights of dazzling white ibis and heron, gloomy, light pierced reaches of forests and sweeping views of the marshes—the undulating merger of earth and water which gives this landscape its unearthly dimension of mystery.

5. A walkway spans the marsh on Sapelo

6. *(above)* Marsh buggy on
Sapelo Island used by the
University of Georgia
Marine Institute

7. *(left)* A lonely walk
on Blackbeard Island

8. Blackbeard Island

4

Sapelo

A JOURNEY BACK IN TIME

Two hundred years ago, an exiled French royalist, the Marquis de Montalet, led a snorting pig beneath the gnarled, moss-draped oaks of Sapelo Island in a daily search for truffles, a delicacy which he devoutly believed could make men gay, women tender, and might conceivably civilize barbaric America. The gentle little gourmet never found a truffle, but in the end it did not matter. On his deathbed, he whispered to his Negro chef, Cupidon: "We need search no more for truffles, for here all are gentle and tender."

Sapelo, he realized, has its own civilizing properties. Sailing out from the landing north of Darien is like a journey back in time. Egrets, terns, and herons wheel and swoop over vast emerald fields of marsh grass, and the shore line is a tangled thicket of live oak and muscadine vines pierced by a solitary lighthouse. The view from the deck of the ferry *Janet* is virtually the same that greeted the Portuguese sailors who discovered the island in 1520.

The infinite forest has erased all but a few traces of the past. Nothing remains of the original Creek settlers but two Indian burial mounds and a mysterious ceremonial ring of oyster shells which archaeologists estimate to be 3500 years old. The tabby mission, built by the Jesuit missionaries in 1567 and later occupied by the Franciscans, is gone now. Vines shroud the crumbling ruins of Le Chatelet, the Marquis' plantation home which the Negroes still call "Chocolate," and Burning Bull, the tabby church that dates back to "slavery time," is scarcely visible in the undergrowth. Across the creek, on Blackbeard Island, a single gun emplacement is all that remains of the bloody reign of the pirate who claimed to be the devil's brother, and a crumbling brick crematory is a grim reminder of the era when the island was a quarantine station for yellow fever victims. Even the palatial pink stucco "Big House" on Sapelo is empty now—deer drink from the fountains and cardinals flash through the heavy veils of Spanish moss.

On the mainland, they will warn you that Sapelo is haunted. If it's true, few islands can claim a more colorful band of phantoms. Among the first settlers was Pedro Menendez, the scholarly Jesuit of San Jose Mission, who christened the island Guale in 1606 and authored the first book ever written in America—a little grammar in the Yamassee tongue for the Indian children of the island.

A hundred years later came the pirate Blackbeard, lurching into battle with a two-foot cutlass clenched in his teeth, his beard ablaze with burning hemp. He made the abandoned mission his lair, and, legend has it, beheaded his sixteenth wife and six members of his crew and buried them in a shroud of gold doubloons on the island that they still call Blackbeard, the island just across Cabretta Sound from Sapelo. A wildlife preserve since 1800, Blackbeard today is lovingly tended by Ranger Sam Vickery, who swims alongside alligators in one of two freshwater lakes, protects the thousands of ducks that flock there every fall, and tends the magnificent eight-mile beach that stretches the length of the island and terminates abruptly in a weird, spectral forest of driftwood. In the dark heart of Blackbeard's splendid climax forest, Vickery can point out the spike in a shattered oak that is said to mark the pirate's treasure, but no one has ever found it. One band of hunters swears that when they unearthed the anchor chain of the chest, they were struck by a bolt of lightning and attacked by six headless men brandishing flaming swords. Another group of treasure seekers returned to Jacksonville and told a New York *Times* reporter they had been attacked by a fire-breathing bull. They had, the *Times* duly noted, the burns to prove it. "Only me and the Devil knows where that treasure is," Blackbeard used to say darkly, "and it'll go to the one who lives the longest."

After the Revolution, General Francis Hopkins, a descendant of the Tuscan nobility, built his home on the north end of the island. His son John, a trigger-tempered fighter given to drawing stingingly funny cartoons, killed McQueen McIntosh in a duel that is still hotly debated in Darien. Jailed for murder, Hopkins protested his innocence in a heart-wrenching diary—"I am the most desolate of men," he wrote before he escaped and fled to England, where he masqueraded as a surgeon with alarming success for three years. Later he donned the robes of a Superior Court judge and slipped quietly into Tennessee where he was ambushed and killed at the age of thirty-three.

Five French royalists purchased the island in 1790, among them the Marquis de Montalet, the Santo Domingo planter who had owned Savannah's legendary Hermitage. Renowned for his extraordinary cuisine, the Marquis devoted himself to training his Negro chef and rewarded him with the cordon bleu when he had mastered such delicacies as purée of artichoke and poulard in olive oil with sweet cream. But while the Marquis searched for truffles and established the island's tradition of sumptuous hospitality, his fellow exiles found little but tragedy on Sapelo. Their bitter disputes finally led to the duel that killed one member and ended their idyll in the New World.

The reign of the Scotsman, Thomas Spalding, heir to the Barony of Ashantilly, began in 1800 and proved to be the island's golden era. He introduced Sea Island cotton, ran a thriving sugar mill, and grazed a herd of blooded Aberdeen Angus bulls. His enterprises flourished under the scrupulous eye of a North African slave, Bu Allah, a devout Moslem who paused three times a day to kneel on his sheepskin prayer rug and bow to the East. Spalding's slaves were treated so well that the island was called "Nigger Heaven" by Darien mainlanders. Spalding himself trusted them enough to break all precedent by arming them with muskets during the War of 1812. The dour, benign Scotsman dominated the island from the tabby house called South End Place, helped forge the Georgia constitution, and served a term as a U.S. congressman. He did not live to see his barony destroyed by the

Civil War, but his sons returned from battle to find South End in ruins, the slaves scattered, and the fields wasted.

Sapelo did not recover from the war until the twenties, when the island was purchased by a Detroit auto magnate, Howard Coffin. On the ruins of South End Place, he built a stunning pink stucco palace, improbable as a dream with its crystal fountains and its Italian marble nymphs, its fabled ballrooms and muraled indoor pool. Coffin's lavish balls and midnight suppers, often graced by the taciturn presence of President Calvin Coolidge or the young Charles Lindbergh, were the delight of the slicker fashion magazines which reported them in florid detail. R. J. Reynolds, the last owner of the "Big House," followed the Sapelo tradition of extravagant hospitality. Reynolds realized that Sapelo's future lay with the sea, and before his death, he created the foundation designed to preserve the island for research and presided over the birth, in 1954, of the University of Georgia's Marine Institute.

Today, Sapelo's future is guided by modern day Jeremiahs like Dr. Eugene Odum, the father of modern ecology, whose doctrine, while purely scientific, derives from Dr. Albert Schweitzer's profound understanding that "the great fault of all ethics has been that they believed themselves to have to deal only with the relationship of man to man." No one understands better than Dr. Odum that if man is not to follow the whooping crane's tragic flight to extinction, he must develop the reverence for life which is the foundation of modern ecology, the study of man's complex dependence on a bewildering variety of other creatures and life processes.

Co-author of the standard college textbook *Fundamentals of Ecology*, and a specialist in estuarine marshes, Dr. Odum

[77]

has been an indefatigable champion of an over-all plan for the Georgia coast, a plan which would zone Brunswick and Savannah for industry, preserve Sapelo as a research park, and protect the other islands as natural areas. He has fought for a marshbank to preserve the marshes intact for research and appropriate leasing, for open-areas legislation, and for public understanding of man's complex and infinitely dependent relationship with the marshes and the sea.

He recognizes, perhaps better than any other ecologist in the nation today, that "to pull one thread is to unravel the entire tapestry." On the Georgia coast, man's predatory tampering with his environment has resulted in the over-harvesting which has killed Georgia's once flourishing oyster industry. The coastal marshes, a vital barricade against hurricanes and the key to the future of Georgia's marine culture, are endangered by capricious road planning, back filling, and the lowering of water tables by insatiably thirsty coastal industries. Another imminent danger: on some of the sea islands, shielded by splendid climax forests and ringed with virgin beaches, rights have been sold for the strip mining of low-grade phosphates—the actual mining operations have been blocked by outraged citizens' groups armed with a carefully documented study of the coastal ecology prepared by the Marine Institute scientists who have become razor-sharp vigilantes of the estuaries.

Dr. Odum has been in the front ranks of this battle, trying to re-educate a public whose judgments are based on economics, progress, and development to the fact that man has passed his growth stage and entered an era of perilous maturity. "We have been a consumptive, destructive civilization," he tells citizens' groups throughout the state. "We must now learn to recycle and reuse." More important than the race to the moon is the life or death race for environmental stability and balance, for total planning and for recycling wastes and pollutants—man's vast and ultimately self-destructive litter on the earth.

The estuaries—the marshes, the sand and mud flats, the creeks and bays, where salt water mingles with fresh, are the most productive acreage known to man. As a nutrient trap and a nursery for fish, one acre of marsh, the biological heart of the estuary, may produce ten tons of organic matter in a year. While other nations use the estuaries to support their human population, Americans value them only for sewers or land development; but destroy the marshes and the islands are lost, warns this new Jeremiah.

He and the Institute scientists are leading Sapelo into an era of ecological sophistication which promises to enlighten the entire nation. Their laboratories are quartered in a quadrangle of buildings which were once the Reynolds' dairy complex, but their equipment ranges from a sixty-five-foot research vessel, the *Kit Jones*, to an improbable-looking piece of machinery called a marsh buggy which cores the salt marsh for sedimentological analysis. Three resident scientists are doing basic research on the geological evolution of the southeastern Atlantic coast, studying the relationship of ancient shore lines in Utah to the Georgia coast and cataloguing the origins, sediments, and animal life found in the salt marsh. Other scientists are studying pollution ecology, the physiology and ecology of fish and marine microbiology. But the research most vital to Georgia's economy is in the field of oyster cultivation. The state's oyster industry, once the nation's largest, has been all but destroyed by over harvesting, jeopardizing the entire coastal economy. Thus the institute has enlisted the aid of two oyster propagation specialists from Japan who are perfecting production techniques appropriate to the Georgia coast. Among the most promising: the "raft culture" method in which long lines of oyster shells are strung out between floating barrels to act as a substrate on which fledgling oyster crops can thrive. Dr. James Henry, who heads the Institute, believes this may well be the technique that will rejuvenate the Golden Isles' oyster industry.

At Sapelo, the Institute's nine resident scientists live like colonialists in concrete-block, jalousied bungalows overlooking the salt marsh. They keep rigid hours, governed by the ebb and flow of the tides, educate their children in a one-room, six-grade school, import prime steaks and a modest ration of bourbon from the mainland, and traverse the island's eight miles of deeply rutted roads in rebuilt jeeps equipped with snakebite kits. Remembering the Sunday one scientist caught three deadly lemon sharks in an hour of surf casting, they shy away from the beach and swim in the pool near the guest house they call Ashantilly. During the day they can be found taking tide samples on the deck of the *Kit Jones* or plunging through the deeper reaches of the marsh on the buggy, drilling for core samples which are examined for clues to the geologic history of the great barrier islands. At night they cross the grass-tossed dunes to the "big pond" and gather tiny luminous fish which shimmer like fireflies in coils of net. The marsh and the sea are their laboratories; as they compile their endless catalogues of Sapelo's teeming marine life, they are writing a history that dates back to creation and anticipates tomorrow.

But while the scientists look to the future, the Negroes, descendants of the Spalding slaves, dwell in a strange twilight between the present and the past.

At the windowless shack they call Benny's Confectionery, Allan Greene, the sage of Blackbeard Island, weaves a wicker basket and philosophizes on the mysterious ways of God. "I figures He created sandflies to keep the damnyankees from taking over the South," he says. Sipping a tepid can of beer, young George Walker, the Institute's crack mechanic, recounts the story of a cousin who was acquitted of murder at the exact moment his aunt muttered an incantation and released a chicken from her yard. Down the road in a cabin behind the watermelon patch, ancient Allen Walker settles back in a cane-bottom chair and recalls in a soft but almost unintelligible Gullah accent, how his mother brought water to the field hands during "slavey time." Affectionately he recites the names of his schoolteachers—Charlie Gwin, Rosa Polite, Professor Jeremiah Walker. He explains that "first, in the beginning my grandfolk were called Worker, but it was changed to Walker," and he remembers the rosin still and the oyster factory and the rice mill on Doboy Island. "The time is now just like a few passing days," he says, "all happiness and pleasure," but he grows nostalgic for the old church at Hanging Bull—"It was a great enjoyment to this island." The later church, the church at Raccoon Bluff, which is almost deserted now, is confusing to him. "When I go down there it seems like a dream to me. I open the door and the people who went there are all growed up and gone away. You think of the people you used to know and you just gets all confused . . ."

Not long ago, Allen Walker moved his membership to the

other church on Sapelo, St. Luke's Baptist at the South End, where prayer meeting is held every other night. The women sit on one side of the aisle, the men on the other, in varnished pews stirring the hot, heavy air with funeral parlor fans. Sam Hillary, reading from the Bible in the thin light of a goose-necked lamp, intones the 121st psalm—"I will lift up mine eyes unto the Lord. . . ." The men chant an old hymn, "I will trust in de Lord," while Mother Dixon kneels at her pew and prays, in an achingly sweet, rich voice: "Our Almighty and Everlasting Father, we thank thee for the sun that rises in the East and sets in the West. . . . Realizing Father that thou art God, help us to behold another beautiful day . . . Father, we all has a great need for thee . . . We are down here in great distress. . . ."

The dissonant ghosts of Sapelo, the inscrutable Creeks and the gentle Spanish monks, the pirates and the great planation lords, the Yankee industrial barons and the new aristocracy of scientific intellectuals seem to speak in a single voice as she prays on, counting, like a rosary, the beads of human sorrow and eternal hope.

"Remember, Lord, the trouble of this old world, remember our boys on the chain gang and our boys in Vietnam . . . Know that we are still struggling for survival, traveling through this old unfriendly world . . . Bring us, Holy Father, in thy good time, into one big family. . . ."

"Amen," murmurs the congregation. "Amen."

5

Midway Church

PIETY AND THE CHRIST CRAZE

"Old Midway is not really dead, she lives in her children," the pastor, Reverend James Stacy, affirmed on May 8, 1889, as he addressed the congregation in the dooryard of the austere little church that stands, like a staunch New England pilgrim, among the voluptuous magnolias and veiled oaks at Midway.

The congregation, dispersed and impoverished by the Civil War, had gathered to replace the cornerstone, laid in 1754, that had been rifled and demolished by the "Gospel Army" who had used the church as a slaughterhouse, butchering meat on the melodeon in the last, cruel days of "The War."

The freed slaves had fallen heir to the church, planters like the LeContes had gone west, and the railroad had come, introducing what the Reverend Mr. Stacy darkly referred to as "foreign elements." The parish that had produced two signers of the Declaration of Independence, four Georgia governors, six foreign missionaries and eighty-two ministers had already begun what Stacy called "the gradual but certain departure from the Puritan strictness and piety of their faithful ancestry." And, though the gentle pastor did not know it, Midway Church was even then on the threshold of the strangest phenomenon in this nation since the Salem witch hunts of 1692—the Christ Craze, a theatrical and outrageously fraudulent second coming staged by a fanatical Ohio Yankee shrewd enough to realize that when the Saviour did come, no congregation would be better prepared to receive him than pious Midway.

Today the Midway Museum, a colonial manse flanked by noble chimneys, displays the cherished artifacts—the handmade silver, the English pewter and the communion goblets used by the congregation that was known throughout the nation for its military daring in three wars and its missionary zeal in evangelizing the coastal slaves. Cherokee roses smolder on the crumbling brick wall that cloisters the Midway dead whose witness, vowed the Reverend Mr. Stacy, "lingers like holy fragrance around this sacred spot." The magnificent iron gate, a gift of the legendary Liberty County Troop, is rusting now. They will lend you the key at the Gulf Station on Highway 17 where the turpentine workers gather to sip Nehi in the afternoons. In the shadow of the obelisk which honors Midway's Revolutionary heroes, General Screven and General Stewart, lie hundreds of marble slabs, their aching lyrics blurred by pink lichens and moss. But the profile of a people, a ghostly company of the devout, is distinguishable still.

There is John Stacy, Born December 10, 1761, Died April 7, 1818.

> His religion was without ostentation
> His zeal without bigotry,
> His friendship without pretense . . .

Here sleeps Mrs. Mary Ham (1790–1826)

> Forgive, best shade, the tributary tear
> That mourns thy exit from a world like this
> Forgive the wish that would have kept thee here
> And stayed thy progress to a seat of bliss.

And Ann Evelyn Robarts. 13 May 1794–15 September 1811

> Best and fairest of thy sex, alas farewell
> from this dark scene removed to shine
> Where purest shades of mortals dwell
> And Virtue waits to welcome thine.

And here too rests one of the prophets of the church known as "the Cradle of Liberty"—Joseph Quarterman (1764–1801)

> Lo; Where this silent marble weeps
> A friend, a husband, father sleeps
> A heart within whose sacred cell
> The peaceful virtues loved to dwell . . .

In the long and perilous exodus to their promised land at Midway, the congregation often compared itself to Moses and the Israelites. They were, as the Honorable W. E. Law pointed out at the great Centennial of 1854, "the intellectual and moral nobility of the province of Georgia . . . men who had been tried, who had left their homes and all for conscience sake and come to this country that they might enjoy freedom in the worship of God. . . . men of the deepest religious convictions, courage and resolution, not afraid of hardships and sufferings. . . ."

The exodus began in England, in 1630, when a band of 140 Congregationalists—natives of Somersetshire, Devon, and Dorset counties—sailed on the chartered ship *Mary and John* to join the Congregationalist sect which the Reverend Samuel Skelton had established in Salem, Massachusetts in 1629, the sect which was to be notorious for its persecution of witches. Their Moses, the Reverend John Warham, "expounded the word daily" during their stormy seventy-day passage to New England where, near Boston, they laid out the village of Dorchester, the nomadic name they retained when, sixty-five years later, they moved to South Carolina in search of more land. A congregation avowedly "militant and missionary" by then, they settled on the Ashley River, eighteen miles from Charleston, where in February 1696 they held the first sacrament of the Lord's Supper ever celebrated in Carolina. It was here that the congregation, bowing to the inexorable demands of lowland rice culture, became slaveowners. By 1742, the young, eager to extend their holdings, were once more searching for a new and richer promised land; the exodus was not yet over. They turned south again, to the "Medway swamp and adjacent lands" on the Georgia coast, 40 miles below Savannah, where they were granted 22,400 acres of land by Georgia officials of the crown—five hundred acres to each settler with four hundred acres set aside for a glebe, an appropriation for the church.

The Midway settlers, 280 whites and 536 slaves, arrived

on July 11, 1752, and two years later celebrated the Lord's Supper on the road that led to Sunbury—the burgeoning port, a veritable Sodom and Gomorrah with "no religious instruction at all," according to the pious Midwayites. From the beginning, the religious community was governed democratically. In the Articles and Rules of Incorporation, adopted in August of 1754, they vowed that as a "dissenting" church, they must "lay a foundation by the blessing of God, of peace and harmony among ourselves."

It was in this spirit that the little company of Congregationalists sustained a baptism of suffering—of sickness, privation, and Indian attack which Midway pastors have compared to "Israel in the wilderness, the covenanters of Scotland, the Huguenots of France, Moses at Medea or Paul at Arabia."

But they remained militant dissenters. Representatives from Midway served on the committee which drafted the first Revolutionary resolution adopted at the historic meeting at Tondee's Tavern in Savannah in August of 1774. The sanctuary was garrisoned by a fortification and its cavalry, the Independent Troop, was the first in the state—two reasons, perhaps, why the sanctuary was desecrated and burned by the British under General Augustin Provost after the unconditional surrender of the garrison at Sunbury. Both General Screven and General Stewart died defending Midway, and the Reverend Moses Allen, who preached Midway's first sermon in Georgia, was taken prisoner at the fall of Savannah and drowned in the waters off Sunbury after escaping from a British ship; the captain indignantly refused to grant any boards for his coffin.

Ravaged by the Revolution, it was 1784 before the community assembled to plan a "coarse meeting house" to stand near the site of the burned church. By 1792 the permanent sanctuary had been built—a stark, proud New England church of whitewashed cypress with green, shuttered windows and a piercing steeple that was to become a symbol of piety to the nation. Tiny gold plates on the hinged door of each pew identified the lessee and the gallery was given over to the slaves, who had been holding their own worship services in the woods across the Sunbury Road. A Freedman who lived on Peter Winn's plantation—they called him Mingo —preached from a raised platform in a booth, assisted by Mr. Salter's Jack, who was later purchased by the church.

Midway, even then, was known for its virtue. The community had never had a homicide; theft and crime were unknown and drunkenness was rare—the good ladies of the congregation like Mrs. Quarterman were known to substitute cologne for rum in their Christmas eggnog. Sunday services began at eleven in the unheated building and continued until four, when the planters rode home to spend the evening instructing their children in the catechism.

The strong hold of the church on their lives was due, believes Mr. Stacy, "to their intense scrupulousness to meet all their pecuniary obligations, especially what they owed their minister . . . to family worship; to the hearty endorsement of the Abrahamaic Covenant, the thorough religious training and discipline of the children, strict observance of the Sabbath day, and the entire absence of anything like religious excitement." But he also added that Midway, cradle not only of liberty but of innocence, was "almost totally isolated from the rest of the world . . . and all the temptations and frivolities of modern life."

The workings of the Holy Ghost were often awesome and majestic. A camp meeting in December of 1830 evoked such an intensity of spiritual zeal that the planters sent home for provisions and bedding, slept on the frozen ground and worshiped from dawn to midnight. "It was prayer, praise, exhortation and preaching, either in private tents or in the public sanctuary," Stacy recalls. "The very ground seemed holy. I remember one cold night the whole congregation were on their knees, supplicating mercy for themselves and others. It was one of the most remarkable revivals that ever occurred in Georgia." There are records of other December meetings "that shook the strongholds of Satan."

Among this blazing company of the devout, there was only one who doubted, Macon Baker, on whose tomb is inexorably inscribed: "Though clearly marked as an early victim of the tomb, he was not a professor of religion." The agony of his disbelief is recorded in a poem he wrote in November 1852, shortly before his death.

> May I not yet hope to see Thee
> Heavenly Father, God of Love?
> Wilt thou not, oh Father free me
> From my guilt, my sin remove.

From the beginning, the "house Negroes" of Midway shared Communion with their masters. Says Dr. Mallard in a little book written in the early nineteenth century: "the number of black communicants is so large that Tony Stevens comes from the gallery to replenish the gold-lined silver goblets from the basket of wine in bottles near the pulpit; and as the wine is poured out, its gurgling in the solemn silence smiles distinctly upon our young ears and the whole house is filled with the aroma of the pure, imported Madeira . . . A prayer, doxology and benediction close the solemn and impressive service, solemn and impressive as nowhere else."

But on the rice plantations there were vast numbers of Negroes who knew nothing of the saving grace of Midway until Dr. Charles C. Jones organized the "Midway Church Missionary Society," one of the first groups in the country to evangelize the slaves. "Let it be proclaimed with the voice of a trumpet that churches which live only for themselves shall die to themselves; no, let the word be altered, they shall die within themselves," he proclaimed at Midway sanctuary. But when he began his pioneer work among some four thousand slaves in December 1832, he faced a stormy opposition.

The planters were afraid that the large assemblages on Sundays would turn into riots and that night meetings on the isolated plantations would end in "theft, lewdness and carousals." Any attention to the spiritual life of the Negroes would make them "presumptuous, unruly and unprofitable," they argued. And there were dire predictions that the movement would "open the door for improper teachers" and "ruin the country." South of Midway, at Butler's Island, the English actress Fanny Kemble caustically surveyed the great experiment in evangelism and made a more accurate prediction. ". . . the light that they are letting in between their fingers will presently strike them blind and the mighty flood of truth which they are straining through a sieve to the thirsty lips of the slaves will sweep them away like straws from their cautious moorings and overwhelm them in its great deeps, to the waters of which man may in nowise say, thus far shall ye come and no farther," she prophesied in her *Journal of a Residence on a Georgian Plantation.*

There was little precedent for Reverend Jones's work. In 1727, the Bishop of London published a "Letter to the Masters and Mistresses of families on the English Plantations Abroad," exhorting them to "encourage and promote the instruction of their negroes in the Faith." The first African conversion to the Protestant religion was not made until 1758 when John Wesley received into the faith a slave woman whose name is unrecorded; her master was Nathaniel Gilbert, a wealthy West Indian planter. And when George Whitefield made his last visit to Savannah, he was accompanied by a Methodist missionary who was to evangelize the slaves. But cotton and Methodism entered Georgia at the same time, and the faithful were soon looking to the writings of St. Paul for Biblical sanctification for the institution of slavery.

The Gospel itself was considered dangerous, especially when interpreted by what one Methodist, W. P. Harrison, called "the heaven-daring impiety of the New England fanatics . . . who would have doomed the early church to extinction . . . and renounced St. Paul, the Bible and the God of Heaven."

Insurrections were often attributed to the incendiary influence of the Gospels. One witness to the 1816 Charleston slave insurrection observed that "a few appeared to have been activated by the instinct of the most brutal licentiousness and by the lust for plunder; but most of them by wild and fanatic ideas of the rights of man and the misconceived injunction of Holy Writ." And when this was followed by yet another insurrection in 1822, Benjamin Elliott concluded that, "the assemblages for religious instruction have been used to instill sentiments of ferocity by falsifying the Bible."

Slaves like Andrew, who dared to preach the gospel in Savannah, were brutally persecuted. Twice he was imprisoned in the Savannah jail and in 1788 he and his brave and zealous little congregation of fifty slaves were publicly flogged with the cat-o'-nine-tails. Bleeding from his wounds, his body lacerated, Andrew proclaimed that he rejoiced in the suffering he endured for his Christ, a declaration of faith so stirring and incandescent that his chastened master gave him a barn on his Brampton plantation to use as a sanctuary. Here he was ordained on the twentieth of January, 1788, by the Reverend Abraham Marshall, who confirmed his congregation of seventy slaves, the genesis of Savannah's First African Baptist Church.

While Christianity could be inflammatory, it could also humble the dissenting spirit if it was interpreted in the light of Pauline doctrine. The converted slave, reported one minister at a South Carolina Methodist Conference in 1832, "is contented with his lot, cheerful in his labors, submissive, for conscience sake, to plantation discipline, happy in life, hopeful in death and from his lowly cabin carried at last by the angels to Abraham's bosom."

This was to be the experience of the Reverend Mr. Jones, but in his hands the gospels were as hard a taskmaster for the owner as for the slave. "Remember that God is their absolute owner and you have but a derived and limited property in them" he admonished the Midway slaveholders in his book on *The Religious Instruction of the Negroes in the U.S.*, published in 1843. "Make it your chief end in buying and using slaves to win them to Christ and save their souls . . . woe to them that by their cruelty and covetousness do scandalize even slaves and hinder their conversion and salvation."

He managed to side-step the dichotomy between the shackles of slavery and the liberating message of the gospels by drawing a strict line between civil and spiritual responsibility, a cruelly ambivalent doctrine which was to characterize the whole realm of southern Protestantism for one hundred years. Acting on his advice, the Presbyterian Synod of South Carolina and Georgia resolved in 1833 "that in the discharge of duty we separate entirely the Civil and Religious conditions of the people, while we devote ourselves entirely to the improvement of the latter, we disclaim all interference with the former."

Ignoring the objections of New England abolitionists who questioned the essential humanity of separating the civil from the religious, the zealous Reverend Jones addressed himself to evangelizing a people who by law were condemned to illiteracy and who, in the isolation of the rice fields, clung to their ancient African rituals of tribal dances and nature worship. In eight Sunday schools, from Sunbury to Sand Hills, he introduced his "pagan" students to the hymnology, the scriptures and systematic theology; by 1845, 647 Midway slaves were dutifully reciting Dr. Jones's catechism, which was later translated into Chinese and used by Presbyterian missionaries throughout Asia.

The Midway settlers believed the gospel transformed their slaves, and it did, but they never really understood the African's mystical and impassioned acceptance of the risen Christ, the Messiah of the wretched, the dispossessed, and the helpless. In the little praise houses in the remote reaches of the rice fields, they translated Reverend Jones's systematic theology into their own ecstatic celebration of the divine— the African rituals of the holy dances around the altar, the holy kisses and the elemental poetry of the "shout"—on New Year's Eve, after a night of singing and praying, they would greet the first frail dawn of the New Year with their own primitive hymn—"Ha'k 'E Angel, Day Oh, See Day a Coming . . ."

Their masters, who regarded religion as an exercise in morality, industry and servility, used the praise house deacons as watchmen, "a mounted police," Joseph LeConte wrote in his autobiography, "that regularly patrolled the country by night and arrested all who were without passes" and strictly imposed the prohibition laws. So stringently were the new converts policed that crime and disorder were almost abolished and runaways, which had totaled fifteen or twenty in a planting season, were no longer attempted. "What hath God wrought?" wrote Midway's pastor, the Reverend Robert Quarterman in January 1844. "Drunkenness, theft, falsehood, profaneness and even lewdness" had been banished, as had "that filthy and disgusting squalidness, that utter indifference to even the common decencies of life which so generally prevailed in former times . . . Indeed they are in all respects a more decent, orderly and morally respectable people. And Joseph LeConte recalled that he had never seen a "happier working class."

Firmly undergirded by slavery, the aristocracy of Liberty County flourished, a righteous company of Renaissance men who seem never to have questioned the institution which produced their golden age. Regard Louis LeConte, master of Woodmanston. His son paints a vivid picture of him strolling through his celebrated gardens, his breakfast cup of coffee in his hands, to inspect his camellia trees, "the largest of these a double white with a thousand blossoms open at once, each blossom four or five inches in diameter, snow white and double to the center," his son wrote. Botanists from all over the North and Europe made pilgrimages to LeConte's gardens, to sample the unique LeConte pears and join his long excursions into the Altamaha region to collect rare plants. He was a master of the classics, higher mathematics, and chemistry and, according to his son, a "just, wise and kindly" keeper of his 200 slaves who "were strongly attached to him and proud of calling him master."

By 1854, when the Midway congregation gathered to celebrate its Centennial, the blessing of the Holy Spirit seemed abundant. The little church had dispatched two missionaries to China and its pastors—men like Dr. Abiel Holmes, father of Oliver Wendell Holmes, and Dr. Samuel Morse, father of the inventor of the electric telegraph, had won national acclaim.

"Hail, venerated country, in this wide world the most venerated spot to me!" exulted the Honorable W. E. Law in his Centennial address. He acclaimed Midway a community of "excellent internal government and police and mutual confidence among citizens . . . the kindest intercourse . . . brotherly love . . . a surface everywhere dotted with houses of worship and schools for the instruction of youth. Temperance, sobriety and truth, a model and example for her sister counties in Georgia." And thirty-five miles away in Savannah, Midway's invalid pastor, the Reverend S. J. Cassels, sat up in bed and drank a solitary toast to "Liberty

County, the place of my first and second birth, yet to be the place of my third."

The war brought a tragic end to the idyll. Liberty County sent two cavalry troops to join the Army of Northern Virginia and the women and children were left to eke out an existence in the abandoned rice fields. In 1864, the great old houses were ravaged by the Federal troops of Colonel Kilpatrick, the silverware was stolen, and families like the Hopkins, who refugeed inland, lived for months on the corn which their former slaves salvaged from the troughs, the slender leavings of Kilpatrick's horses. Midway Church was used as a camping ground, and the cemetery was grazed by cattle, which were slaughtered on the melodeon in the sanctuary. When the survivors of the Independent Troop returned from war, they found nothing but destruction. Colonel Leaner L. Varnedoe, eying his first meal after his return, remarked, with characteristic Liberty County aplomb, "Annie, if you can, you may, but I can't say grace over such a dinner."

When the white families abandoned their plantations, the Negroes took over Midway Church with the blessing of their former masters. A former slave, the Reverend Joseph Williams, was named pastor in 1868 and was soon joined by a white minister, the Reverend J. T. H. Waite, a graduate of Columbia Theological Seminary. In 1889, the two spent a memorable summer trying to restore the breath of Midway sanity to the strange and terrifying phenomenon known today as the Christ Craze.

Dupont Bell, a white man with a flowing beard, his sandy hair falling in ringlets over the shoulders of his copper-colored suit, appeared in the remote pine barrens of Liberty County on a June midnight, knocked on the door of a little

9. Storied Christ Church on St. Simons Island

10. *(left)* Kneeling at altar rail at Harlem Road Church of God

11. *(below)* Bessie Jones demonstrates the bass clap

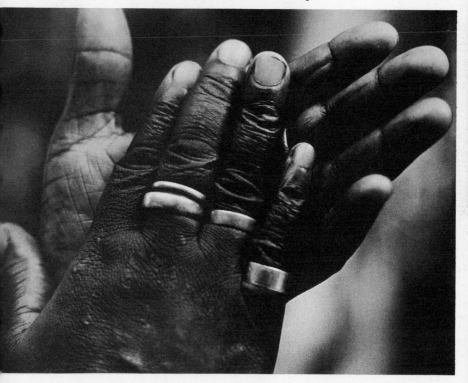

12. Folk singer Bessie Jones

Negro shanty and announced to the startled owner that he
was the Risen Christ, come to proclaim his mission in the low
country.

The next morning the Negro community assembled to
hear the self-appointed Saviour affirm, "I am the Christ who
has been crucified and risen from the dead. Do you remember
the great earth quake of 1886?" They did, with a lingering
shudder of fear and awe. "Were you not shaken at that time?"
"Amen," they replied, recalling that the very earth had trem-
bled, collapsing their flimsy shanties and felling sturdy pines.
"That shaking was produced by my coming," Bell assured
them. "You have been praying for my coming. Now I am
come and there is no need to pray any more, no need to
plant, no need to do anything but get ready."

The world, he announced, would come to an end in
August, when he would lead them, the devout of Midway,
to Jerusalem. He prophesied that the white leadership of
Liberty County would soon rise against him, subject him to
a Sanhedrin court, and cast him out as before, but this time
he would be delivered by his chosen people. When Bell's
flock swelled to almost 23,000 believers, a white man named
Walthour, who was convinced of his authenticity, invited
them to meet in a field beneath the towering oaks at his
"Homestead Place." Here, in a wooden box they called "the
Ark," Bell's disciples deposited their meager savings. Money
was useless now in the last hours of time, said their Saviour,
and anyone who touched the Ark would be smitten by the
Lord.

The Ohio Christ was a blazing preacher, a master of the
Scriptures and a worker of miracles. Walking beneath the
straggly pines on the Riceboro Road one day, he recalled

how Christ had turned the water into wine; then he whipped out a half-dollar, placed it in a tin bucket, shook it, turned it upon the ground and lo, a dollar rolled out. The miracle was talked about by the credulous Gullahs from the pine barrens to the great salt marsh. The Ohio Christ was indeed the son of God; Judgment Day was at hand. The Negroes ceased to plant cotton; they neglected their pumpkins and corn, sold their chickens and hogs, and lived on the proceeds in a sweet, sensuous, fevered July twilight of the gods. In the new dispensation, the disciples existed in a state of mystical ardor which the Reverend Mr. Stacy, the biographer of Midway, could only regard as mass insanity.

The "Christ," as he had prophesied, had his Sanhedrin court. A warrant for vagrancy was sworn out against Bell, who was arrested and brought to the McIntosh station in a buggy flanked by armed men to be tried before the magistrate, Captain W. A. Fleming. As he was carried back to Midway in chains, the multitudes followed him along the dusty road, beneath the livid crepe myrtle, shouting, singing and mourning, "This is our Jesus who was nailed to the tree." The magistrate, looking on, quickly amended the charge from vagrancy to lunacy.

In August of 1889, the month in which he had predicted the world would end, Bell was judged "non compos mentis" and sent to Milledgeville State Hospital for the Insane, where for ten years he preached to a dull-eyed company of the living dead on the black wards.

In a final statement to his flock, Bell had predicted that his spirit would return "in the person and form of a colored man." Magistrate Edward Jones, his right-hand man and counselor, quickly assumed his mantle, and was accepted without question by the faithful who continued to cast their silver into the ark. But Jones had his own Judas, his brother David, who, infuriated by his pretensions of ecclesiastical grandeur, tried to drag him away from a mass meeting in the woods. This led to a frenzied free-for-all, in which at least one disciple was severely beaten. In the general melee, somebody made off with the ark.

When Jones was tried and committed to Milledgeville, Shadrach Walthour, who had been stirred by Bell's tales of Solomon's glory, pronounced himself the risen King Solomon. After a brief, riotous reign, he was arrested for disorderly conduct and jailed at Hinesville, where he died mysteriously —the jailer was tried for murder and acquitted. Next to take the crown of thorns was Ellen Roberts, who proclaimed herself "Queen Mary, Virgin Mary and the Queen of Shebah," and shrewdly went underground, drawing her followers not only from the ranks of the Congregationalists but from the two Baptist churches at Newport and the Methodists at McIntosh. Under her seductive influence, several prominent religious leaders were, according to Stacy, "considerably brought under the influence of this ecclesiastical maelstrom," and went hopelessly insane.

"All restraint seemed to be removed and such orgies and abominations practiced as are hardly to be believed," Stacy reported sadly. "Eye witnesses say that the picture can hardly be overdrawn. Among other things, they were even charged with laying aside the marital vows under the delusive idea of 'having things in common.' But we draw the veil over this part of the proceedings."

In the wake of the Christ Craze, the Negro congregation of Presbyterians built their own church, and Midway was designated a museum. Empty and echoing she stands today. And the cemetery, which the turpentine workers will tell you is haunted, is now under the staunch protection of the Colonial Dames. Historians never mention the Christ Craze, which Stacy recounts with obvious pain—"it is a shame that the glory of Midway must be tarnished," he concluded, forgetting that it was the spiritual ancestors of the credulous, burning, Christ-bitten Congregationalists of Liberty County who launched the Salem witch hunts.

6

Fanny Kemble

AN ACTRESS LOOKS AT SLAVERY

The chimneys of a crumbling lime kiln, set starkly against the vast, salt marsh on Highway 17, mark Butler's Island, the plantation where Fanny Kemble, England's most gifted Shakespearean actress, penned her bittersweet *Journal of a Residence on a Georgian Plantation*, the book which some Georgians still believe prevented England's intervention in the Civil War and determined the defeat of the South.

Only the blue heron and the white ibis frequent the river where the Negro boatmen once sang lusty songs about her fair skin and tiny waist, and the banks once gilded with curtains of yellow jasmine are tangled with thickets. Darien, which she described as a forlorn little town of straggling, tumble-down wooden houses half buried in sand, now boasts a stout fleet of shrimp boats and a Chamber of Commerce—

visitors are welcomed at a candy-striped make-believe river boat with aluminum foil windows and a paddle wheel, which blows up a fine froth of Tide soap on Georgia Day. And the descendants of the slaveholders whom Fanny Kemble derided so caustically will tell you proudly that it was the Scottish Highlanders of Darien who penned the eloquent protest against the introduction of slavery into the colony of Georgia.

But the English actress, who spent only three months here in the winter of 1839, is still hotly debated in the rose-and-damask drawing rooms of the Georgia coast. The descendants of those about whom she wrote—the Butler overseer, Roswell King, for instance—still savor the bitter aftertaste of her description of brutality on the Butler estate. She was, some say tersely, a pathological liar. It is true that her description of the Butler slave cabins—"filthy and wretched in the extreme"—is belied by the writings of Sir Charles Lyell, the British scientist, who in the course of a trip to St. Simons Island in 1845 remarked on the "neat and white washed" Negro homes on Butler's Island. And Dr. Holmes of Darien, the plantation physician whom Fanny Kemble described as shrewd, intelligent, kindly and competent, categorically denied her allegations of squalor and neglect in the infirmary where, she said, "poor wretches lay prostrate on the floor, without bed, mattress or pillow, buried in tattered and filthy blankets." In the Darien *Timber Gazette* of September 13, 1878, the doctor protested, "I plead innocent of any complicity in or knowledge of such things. No doubt the writer believed them, in her utter ignorance of the Negro character and particularly Negro women enceinte who delight in complaints and have a constitutional weakness as to facts. Her great error was in listening to them and looking through morbid glasses upon common plantation events as inhuman and sinful . . ." He defended Pierce Butler as "humane and indulgent almost to a fault" and it is true that after the Civil War the Butler slaves returned to the plantation, pledged their allegiance to their former master, and at his death mourned to his daughter Frances, "Oh missus, our backs is broke."

By her own admission, Fanny Kemble was biased. She confessed to Elizabeth Sedgwick, the New England educator to whom she addressed the letters that make up the *Journal*, that "I am going prejudiced against slavery for I am an Englishwoman in whom the absence of such a prejudice would be disgraceful." ("But," she added, "I go prepared to find many mitigations in the practice of the general injustice and cruelty of the system—much kindness on the part of the masters, much content on that of the slaves; and I feel very sure that you may rely upon the carefulness of my observation and the accuracy of my report of every detail.")

She was also, by her own admission, erratic. She confided to Elizabeth, "the childish excitability" of her temperament: "To follow me through half a day with any species of lively participation in my feelings would be a severe breathless moral calisthenic to most of my friends." And there is reason to believe that her tortured life at Butler's Island—her horror at the dehumanizing effects of slavery, her loneliness among a "barbarous aristocracy," her anguished disillusionment with her husband—drove her to the brink of madness. After she had left Pierce Butler, after she had lost the custody of her daughters in a prolonged, bitter divorce and was living alone in Italy, she wrote a poem "On a young woman who, after a short and wretched marriage, went mad and died."

. . . Mine eyes were put out by ceaseless tears
Blinding them hour by hour and day by day
The hideous vision of my future years
Scared them but once and all was swept away. . . .

The marriage of Fanny Kemble and Pierce Butler represented the ill-starred, cataclysmic alliance of an impassioned
abolitionist and a paternalistic slaveowner, a brilliantly edu-
cated feminist and a simple man who firmly believed a
woman's place was in the home, an ardent idealist who
eschewed the stringent tenets of Calvinism to follow her
own blazing moral imperatives and a husband who regarded
himself as the high priest of his household.

To his faltering, stilted, anguished and bewildered demands
for wifely subservience, she replied in 1842, "It is not in the
law of my conscience to promise implicit obedience to a
human being, fallible like myself, and who can by no means
relieve me of my actions before God." She could not
consider delivering her conscience into her husband's hands.
"Though I love you better than any other living creature,
my affection does not so far blind my judgement as to suggest
you as fit for such a charge," she wrote, a statement which
Butler regarded as ample proof that "Mrs. Butler's opinions,
with regard to the duties of a wife towards her husband,"
were "peculiar and impracticable."

The daughter of England's most celebrated company of
actors, Fanny Kemble had come of age in the lyrical ascend-
ancy of Victorian romanticism—as a schoolgirl in France she
had devoured the poetry of Byron "like an evil potion taken
into my blood." The conscience of her generation was forged
in the flaming moral reaction to the brutalities of the West

India Interest—the handful of planters, slave merchants and bankers who had dominated the British political, economic and social life of the eighteenth century. The torch of abolitionism had finally been taken up by an outraged company of politician spokesmen and propagandists as the newspapers reported such atrocities as the *Zong* case, the notorious slave ship whose captain threw 132 fever-wracked slaves to the sharks in an attempt to place the owner's loss on the underwriters.

At eighteen she already had a strong, sure sense of her literary mission, a deep aversion to acting—"that poor, proletarian profession"—and to the vulgarities of the theatre—the performing animals, the circus acts, and the bland, happy endings which distorted the Shakespearean tragedies she revered. She entered the stage only when Covent Gardens, her father's tragic legacy from her uncle, was covered with bills of sale and the family was on the verge of bankruptcy.

She made her reluctant debut as Juliet on October 5, 1829, and overnight became an idol of the theatre, playing to wildly enthusiastic audiences while Charles Kemble, her Mercutio, slowly began to pay off his debts. In August 1832, the Kembles with Fanny's protective Aunt "Doll" launched a two-year tour of "that dreadful America," and Miss Kemble was immediately hailed in New York as "something of a divine manifestation." She played before Dolly Madison and John Quincy Adams, was presented to President Andrew Jackson and was befriended by America's foremost woman novelist, Catharine Maria Sedgwick, who wrote to Frank Channing in 1833, "we are just now in the full flush of excitement about Fanny Kemble. She is a most captivating creature, steeped to the very lips in genius. I have never seen a woman on the stage to be compared with her."

Fanny Kemble's Juliet also captivated Philadelphia's Butler Mease, who had changed his name to Pierce Butler in compliance with a proviso in his grandfather's will—the will which made him heir, with his brother John, to some 700 slaves on two Georgia plantations, Butler's Island and Hampton on St. Simons Island. His grandfather, a former major in the British Army, had participated in the Constitutional Convention, and was twice elected to the United States Senate and had made a princely fortune on Sea Island cotton before he moved to Philadelphia, abandoning his slaves to the rigid military discipline of his overseer, Roswell King, Sr.

Pierce Butler was an ardent and persistent suitor, following Miss Kemble's appearances from New York to Canada, but she did not accept his proposal of marriage until the sad, soul-searching aftermath of her aunt's death in a stagecoach accident in Canada.

"I know that she preferred his company and conversation to a host of admirers, many of whom had been. . . . more brilliant, but to her appreciation less worthy and sincere," wrote Dr. Holmes, who knew them both intimately. "I remember well the violent antagonisms of his family and best friends, deprecating the misalliance and warning him that it was for his money and not himself . . . but Mr. B. was chosen among others of large if not equal possessions, upon his own merits."

It was not until after their marriage that she discovered he was a slaveowner, or that he realized her abolitionist sympathies. From her honeymoon cottage in Branchtown, a village on the outskirts of Philadelphia, she wrote bitterly, "our present and future fortunes depend greatly upon extensive plantations in Georgia. . . . As for me, though the toilsome earning of my bread were to be my lot again tomorrow, I should rejoice with unspeakable thankfulness that we had not to answer for what I consider so grievous a sin against humanity."

Her spiritual mentor even then was William Ellery Channing, the Unitarian divine who had become a leader of New England liberalism with the publication of his book, *Slavery,* which challenged the Christian to win the soul of the slave-owner and reveal to him the magnitude of his sin—the fact that slavery "crushes the human spirit, denies the dignity of labor, extinguishes the light of reason in man, dissolves the most sacred domestic ties and breeds in master, overseer and driver, cruelty and irresponsibility."

Under his influence, Fanny cast herself as her husband's conscience, composing, on the Branchtown Farm, a vehement treatise against Negro slavery. Pierce Butler finally persuaded her to eliminate it from her first *Journal,* which was published in Philadelphia in the early 1830s, creating a brief, bright literary scandal in England and provoking some astringent reviews from London critics, one of whom compared the author's style to that of a breathless milliner.

Pierce Butler stubbornly opposed Fanny's pleas to visit his Georgia plantation until December 1838 when, with grave misgivings, he embarked with Fanny, their three-year-old daughter Sally, and their infant Fran on the tedious nine-day journey by railroad, coach, and steamboat to remote Butler's Island. When at last the steamer *Ocmulgee* grazed the wharf at Darien, "it seemed to me as if we had touched the outer bound of civilized creation," Fanny wrote. The long gray mourning veils of Spanish moss which shrouded the gnarled live oaks on the river banks struck her as strangely ominous —"the most funereal spectacle in all the vegetable kingdom." And as the Negroes hailed them, "like descending divinities," with whoops and shouts and shrieks of abject joy, she burst into tears.

The family settled into the overseer's austere little house near the rice mill and within sight of one of the four Negro settlements—a cluster of twenty huts, "mere wooden frames pinned, as it were, to the earth by a brick chimney," and dominated by the infirmary. "Here lay those whose health and strength are spent in unrequited labor for us," she wrote. "Here lay women expecting every hour the terrors and agonies of childbirth, others who had just brought their doomed offspring into the world, others who were groaning over the anguish and bitter disappointment of miscarriages —here lay some burning with fever, others chilled with cold and aching with rheumatism, upon the hard, cold ground . . . like brute beasts, absorbed in physical suffering."

As she grappled with an enormous, ragged woman who thrashed convulsively on the floor, quieted another who was barking violently in a fit of epilepsy, and removed a crude poultice of leaves from a foully swollen wound, she wept with pity and wished that "instead of music and dancing and such stuff, I had learned something of sickness and health."

Dr. Holmes denied the terrors she described. Or perhaps these were "the common plantation events" which he felt her "morbid viewpoint" distorted into something "inhuman and sinful."

It is true that Fanny Kemble bridled under every aspect of plantation life, including the "military discipline" which had always prevailed under the regime of Roswell King at Butler's Island. While Dr. Holmes maintained that the lash was seldom used, she reported that "every driver was allowed to inflict a dozen lashes upon any refractory slave in the field, . . . the overseer as many as fifty. And for the master himself, where is his limit? He may, if he likes, flog a slave to death, for the laws which pretend that he may not are a mere pretense, inasmuch as the testimony of a black is never taken against a white."

Nothing in the system she so abhorred was to her more potentially destructive than the family life of the slaves. "The father, having neither authority, power, responsibility or charge of his children, is of course, as among brutes, the least attached to his offspring; the mother by the natural law which renders the infant dependent on her for its first year's nourishment, is more so; but as neither of them is bound to educate or to support their children, all the unspeakable tenderness and solemnity, all the rational and spiritual grace and glory of the connection is lost, and it becomes mere breeding, bearing and suckling. . . ."

She attributed the "reckless increase of the race" to the fact that a woman's labors were lightened when she was pregnant, her food and clothing allowances were increased and she had at least some claim on her master's consideration and good will "for having added to his livestock by bringing a new slave into the world."

Her most heated quarrel with Pierce Butler was over the separation of a Negro family by the sale of Joe, the father, to Roswell King, Jr., who was setting up a plantation of his own in Alabama. Torn with pity for Joe's wife Psyche, and their children, Fanny, as her husband's conscience, tearfully appealed to him "for his own soul's sake . . . not to commit so great a cruelty. . . . I was imploring Mr. (B) to save himself more than to spare these wretched. He gave no answer whatever." But he did, within the course of the day, buy Joe back from Mr. King.

He begged her not to listen to the Negroes who flocked to her with urgent entreaties and pitiful stories, but, she replied, "my conscience forbids my ever postponing their business for any other matter; for with shame and grief of heart I say it, by their unpaid labor I live—their nakedness clothes me, and their heavy toil maintains me in luxurious idleness."

Among the petitioners she noted in a single morning:

"Fanny has had six children; all dead but one. She came to beg to have her work in the field lightened.

"Nanny has had three children; two of them are dead. She came to implore that the rule of sending them into the field three weeks after their confinement might be altered.

"Sophy, Lewis's wife, came to beg for some old linen. She is suffering fearfully; had had ten children; five of them are dead. The principal favor she asked was a piece of meat, which I gave her.

"Sally, Scipio's wife, has had two miscarriages and three children born, one of them is dead. She came complaining of incessant pain and weakness in her back. This woman was a mulatto daughter of a slave called Sophy, by a white man of Walker, who visited the plantation.

"Charlotte, Renty's wife, had had two miscarriages, and was with child again. She was almost crippled with rheumatism, and showed me a pair of poor swollen knees that made my heart ache. I have promised her a pair of flannel trousers, which I must forthwith set about making.

"Sarah, Stephen's wife; this woman's case and history were alike deplorable. She had had four miscarriages, had brought seven children into the world, five of whom were dead, and was again with child. She complained of dreadful pains in the back, and an internal tumor which swells with the exertion of working in the fields; probably, I think, she is ruptured. She told me she had once been mad and had run into the woods, where she contrived to elude discovery for some time, but was at last tracked and brought back, when she was tied up by the arms and heavy logs fastened to her feet, and was severely flogged. . . ."

Sarah recounted this story in a "low, plaintive, monotonous murmur of misery, as if such sufferings were 'all in a day's work,'" wrote Fanny, humbled by the "desperate patience, the patience of utter despair, with which they endured their sorrow-laden existence."

The islanders, convinced that the Negro was inherently false and deceitful, were deeply critical of her credulity. John Couper, one of the few planters whom she admired as a humane and just master, appreciated the Negroes' "sweetness of temper and natural gentleness of disposition," but he also compared them to the Irish in "their subserviency, their flattering, their lying and pilfering." And when she visited Tunno's Island, Dr. Tunno told her quite firmly that "no Negro was to be believed on any occasion on any subject." She herself was leery of repeating the mistakes of Harriett Martineau whose published observations of the South in 1834 were marred because the author "had the misfortune to possess that unsuspecting reliance upon the truth of others which they are apt to feel who themselves hold truth most sacred." She realized that some of the Butler slaves were habitual liars, but she also realized that "the vice results much more from the circumstances in which they are placed than from any natural tendency to untruth in their case."

She worked tirelessly to ameliorate their condition, nursing the sick, encouraging them to learn to read, bribing the children with pennies to wash their faces, whipping up the red cotton dresses they loved and reading prayer services to them on Sundays.

Long after she had left the island, Dr. Holmes recalled her taking the stroke oar of the *Dolphin* when she rowed him over from Darien to care for the sick, racing him to Germantown on Emperor, her splended English hunter, nursing her children with a warmth and tenderness he found surprising in an English woman, reading Shakespeare "in her little island parlor," presiding at a dinner of snipe served with "the old Butler wine." She in turn relished his talk of Darien society, with its social jealousies, its imperceptible shades of respectability, its "delicate divisions of genteel, genteeler and genteelest."

She was openly contemptuous of most of her coastal neighbors, comparing them almost prophetically, to "the nobility of France before the purifying hurricane of the Revolution." She found the men "idle, arrogant, ignorant, dissolute and ferocious, a remnant of barbarism and feudalism." Their pretensions to chivalry, manifested in the *code duello*, disgusted her. When Dr. Hazzard challenged his neighbor John Wylly to a duel after a property dispute, she remarked angrily that, "here nobody is astonished and nobody ashamed

of such preliminaries to a mortal combat between two gentlemen who propose firing at marks over each other's hearts
and cutting off each other's heads." As for the venerated
women of the South: "I pity them for the stupid sameness
of their most vapid existence, which would deaden any
amount of intelligence, obliterate any amount of instruction
and render torpid and stagnant any amount of natural energy
and vivacity. I would rather die, rather a thousand times
—than live the lives of these Georgia planters' wives and
daughters."

With the shrewd perception of the born iconoclast, she
saw through some of their most cherished deceptions. While
they boasted of the cradle to the grave security of slavery,
she compared the lot of the Negro artisans on Butler's Island
to that of Northern artisans "with their white door and
steps, their hydrants of inexhaustible fresh flowing water . . .
the books and newspapers in the little parlor, the daily district
school, the weekly parish church."

And she scoffed at the self-righteous pretensions with which
they tried to absolve themselves of the guilt of slavery. The
efforts of the Midway planters to preach religion to their
slaves was, she said tartly, a subterfuge to make slaves "more
faithful and trustworthy," undertaken with a "safe understanding . . . of what truth is to be given to them and what is
not; how much they may learn to become better slaves and
how much they may not learn lest they cease to be slaves
at all. . . .

"Where shall they begin? 'Whatsoever ye would that men
should do unto you, do ye also unto them'? No, but 'Servants, obey your masters'; and there, I think, they naturally
come to a full stop."

The flamboyant violence, the pretensions to piety and gentility, and the Arthurian code of an aristocracy built on human bondage offended her deepest sensibilities. But she felt an almost holy affinity for the coastal landscape. She loved the noble oaks "like huge, hoary ghosts," the "pale, stiff spikes and fans of dwarf palmetto, the bowers and brakes of the loveliest wilderness where one dares not tread three steps for fear," "the sandy pine barrens, the eternal frame in which all nature is set here," and the infinite fusion of earth and water, undulating, turgid and yellow beneath the incandescent sky like some unearthly outer realm of nature.

She had the poet's unerring eye for detail—the wild plum trees twinkling among evergreen copses, the perfect curtains of yellow jasmine, the butterflies zigzagging in the sun, the dark, lacquered leaves of magnolia grandiflora, the bright golden eye of the Cherokee rose, the exquisite evergreen undergrowth springing up from stagnant, sweltering pools, the "grotesque, laughable flight" of the blue heron, the immovable rows of cranes, "all standing with imperturable gravity upon one leg."

And though she did not realize it, she captured, as no writer ever has, the incredible light of the Georgia coast. "If no human chisel ever yet cut breath, neither did any human pen ever write light; if it did, mine should spread out before you the unspeakable glories of these Southern heavens, the saffron brightness of morning, the blue intense brilliancy of noon, the golden splendor and the rosy softness of sunset. Italy and Claude Lorrain may go hang themselves together! Heaven itself does not seem brighter or more beautiful to the imagination than these surpassing pageants of fiery rays, and piled up beds of orange, golden clouds, with edges too bright to look on . . ."

The coast was to her a tragically beautiful, enchanted land held spellbound by an evil so subtle and insidious that its sweet, somnambulistic effects seduced even men of wisdom and humanity like Dr. Holmes and John Couper. On her return to Philadelphia, she took aim at the dragon and aired her views on slavery in a small work which was to be printed by an abolitionist group and sold at an anti-slavery fair. When Pierce Butler violently opposed its publication, she argued that it was a redemptive act of conscience—"I daily and hourly sacrifice to your perception of right, in my mode of living and the means by which I subsist, all that I think vital in existence—justice, mercy and self respect." But he could only reply in pained resignation, "Few could believe it was out of a husband's power to control his wife in a matter of such importance to their common interests."

Terrified at the impending break-up of his home, he swallowed his pride and wrote to one of Fanny's abolitionist friends. "Twice she has taken her jewels to Philadelphia and sold them in order to obtain money for travel and I have had the mortification of buying them back. What could I do with two little motherless children? And would Fanny be happy parted. . . . and earning her money by public show?" By June, Mrs. Charles Sedgwick was writing Fanny that "your mind is positively and greatly diseased," and to Pierce Butler she mourned, "God who has withheld reason from her, alone can endow her with it now . . . Oh how I weep when she knows it not that a heart so warm and true as hers should be warped by a head so weak."

Through their turbulent quarrels, their painful separations, and doomed and ardent reconciliations on two continents, Fanny maintained, "There are certain prices at which nothing is to be purchased, and the surrender of conscience is a sinful sacrifice, which has no equivalent." But Pierce Butler, schooled in the stultifying tradition of southern chivalry, could only reply, "the dangerous sophistry of such sentiments held by an individual, and that individual a woman, is apparent."

Torn between her deepest convictions and her love for her daughters, she would return after a restless, wretched separation to live in private quarters in Pierce Butler's household, watch helplessly as an English governess was charged with the discipline and education of her children, and communicate with Pierce in cryptic, anguished little notes passed at the silent dinner table. Their final separation came after a bitter quarrel in October 1845; she fled to Rome to immerse herself in art, the religion of her fevered heart, and to recuperate from the crippling sense of bereavement she felt for her daughters. When she returned to the stage, he denied her any further communication with the children. "She wrote what was not true and what was designed and calculated to estrange and prejudice the minds and hearts of my children. In mercy and justice to them, I could not suffer this," he wrote in his privately printed defense of his divorce action.

In England, she captivated British audiences, won dazzling notices for her Shakespearean readings, and earned an international reputation as a poet, diarist, critic, and musician and both shocked and delighted Victorian England by her prowess as a horsewoman and an Alpine climber in Switzerland, which became the second home of her spirit. The circles in which she moved included Sir Walter Scott, Thackeray,

Browning, Lady Byron and Miss Mitford in London, and in Cambridge, Emerson, Lowell, Oliver Wendell Holmes, Longfellow, and Mrs. Beecher Stowe, who vowed, "She would make six clever women and there would be a remnant."

In Philadelphia, Pierce Butler's fortunes turned, and in 1858 some 500 of the Butler slaves were sold in Savannah at the largest auction that city had ever witnessed. As the iron realities of economics threatened the ephemeral idyll of the cotton empire, and the South moved bombastically, stubbornly, and inexorably toward civil war, Fanny Kemble withheld publication of her journal, resisting the impassioned urgings of her abolitionist friends and the immutable press of history. It was not until Lee's defeat at Antietam, when the tide of English sympathy swung toward the South and Lincoln's preliminary emancipation proclamation of September 22, 1862 was derided by the British press as an empty, hypocritical, and vengeful gesture, that she made her decision to publish. When the *Journal of a Residence on a Georgian Plantation* came out in May 1863, the Emancipation Proclamation of January 1 had already ignited the anti-slavery sentiments of the English working classes, who rallied in support of the proclamation at mass meetings throughout the country. But Georgians are still convinced that Fanny Kemble singlehandedly prevented England's recognition of the Confederacy and tipped the precarious balance of power against the South.

The personal cost of her final, wrenching act of conscience was to be immeasurably painful. For it was her youngest daughter Frances, the child whom she idolized, who paid the inevitable price of violence. After Lee's surrender, she could only sit helplessly by in London while Frances shouldered the tragic legacy of Butler's Island. Alone after her father's death, in a conquered nation under military rule, she was left to care for the Butler slaves. Those who had been quartered in the interior struggled home, hungry, ragged, and hopelessly bewildered by the new order, and many of those who had been sold in 1858 used their new freedom to return to their former master. Frances took over the ruined land, supported the old, the indigent and the very young on her father's slender legacy, introduced her wary, suspicious field hands to the wage system, hired a Negro teacher from Philadelphia to instruct both the old and the young, and struggled relentlessly against the cynical oratory of northern politicians to convince her former slaves that freedom meant responsibility and education, not "20 acres, a mule and an umbrella." The eventual success of her ten-year struggle had become a legend among the defeated planters of the coast when the Reverend J. W. Leigh, a visiting Episcopal clergyman from England, discovered her "like a queen among her sable subjects" and fell in love with her.

The two were married and living in London, where he was Dean of Hereford, when Jim Dent, of Hofwyl Plantation, visited them. His daughter, Miss Ophelia Dent, the tiny, gallant, imperishably beautiful mistress of Hofwyl, is perhaps the only woman on the Georgia coast who can claim—though she would never do so—to have the last, revealing word on Fanny Kemble. She is the seventh generation of her family to occupy the gracious frame house on the oak-shadowed bluff overlooking the golden marshes that adjoined Pierce Butler's plantation. Here, among the Jeremiah Theus portraits, the English silver and porcelains of a long and venerable line, she speaks of her father's strange encounter with Fanny Kemble in the drawing room of the Leighs' London home.

It was 1890, and Jim Dent, who had lived through the long, cruel, hunger-haunted aftermath of the war, had no desire to hear Miss Kemble's views on slavery. But when he found himself alone with her before dinner, she disarmed him by demanding to know "what the South thinks of me?"

He did not answer; he had himself forbidden his daughter Ophelia to read her book.

"What I want to tell you," she said gravely, "is that I was a young, impetuous woman then. I would give a great deal now not to have written that book. There has been so much suffering on both sides, so much suffering. . . ."

Three years later, Fanny Kemble was dead, mourned by the leading artists, musicians, writers and statesmen on two continents and more quietly and poignantly by the Alpine guides of Switzerland who called her "la dame qui va chantant par les montagnes." After her death, her son-in-law, who had adored her "superabundant dual nature," her lyrical genius, and her blazing compassion, made a sentimental journey to Butler's Island and found it swept bare by a violent, vagrant tornado that had somehow spared Jim Dent's estate at Hofwyl. He described a scene of utter desolation— "mill and barn had been blown down and all the Negro houses; the plantation house was knocked almost to pieces and our rice crops were completely lost." Nothing remained but the twin chimneys of the lime kiln that still stand today, monuments to the divided heart of a wounded land.

13. Ghosts haunt Eboe Landing on St. Simons

14. Lions guard abandoned
estate at Jekyll

15. A palatial reminder of the Millionaire's Club

7

Tunis Campbell

BLACK SEPARATISM ON
ST. CATHERINE'S ISLAND

The failure of the nation's first great experiment in Black Separatism still mars the haunting beauty of the Georgia coast. The era is forgotten now; historians have deleted it from their texts and if the old-timers remember it, they maintain a tight-lipped conspiracy of silence.

Today, St. Catherine's Island, headquarters of the black empire, sleeps in the white-hot sun across the sound from the dead town of Sunbury. Here, in the sixteenth century, the Spanish Jesuits first converted the drought-starved Creek Indians to Catholicism by inducing, with their mysterious incantations, a blinding miracle of a rainstorm, a storm shot with blazing streaks of lightning that splintered an oak from which the Indians fashioned crosses in awed obeisance to the

Jesuit God. It was here that the Indian half-breed princess, Mary Musgrove, ruled the coastal island Creeks in defiance of British imperialism, and here too that the enigmatic Button Gwinnett settled after he signed the Declaration of Independence. But all that remains are the tabby cabins where the black hierarchy of slaves turned statesmen ruled over the Georgia coast. The wild and shattering beauty of the island, the tortured oak forests, the quivering marshes, the dazzling, deserted beaches yield no hint of the strange kingdom that once flourished here.

The tragic aftermath of Separatism can best be seen in the desolate little enclaves of the coast, in settlements like Tiger Ridge, a colony of angular, misshapen little people, warped and stunted by generations of in-breeding, hunger, and isolation. In their windowless, privy-less shanties, proudly displayed among the accumulated treasures of their generations on this land, are Confederate swords and handsomely framed portraits of aristocratic forebears, surrounded by ten-cent photo-booth pictures of the innocent, disfigured idiots of the clan, inheritors of some monstrous genetic curse. You can see the residue of Separatism too at Daufuskie Island, where ancient, incoherent Gullahs idle away their days in the fitful twilight of syphilitic paresis, the ultimate victims of the golden dream of freedom which was betrayed on the Georgia coast.

The empire, created in January 1865, by virtue of General William T. Sherman's Headquarters Order Number 15, extended from the islands south of Charleston to the St. Johns River and thirty miles inland. This was the domain of Tunis G. Campbell, a tall, suave, copper-skinned former baker's apprentice and Methodist preacher from New Jersey, a man given to gold-rimmed spectacles and high beaver hats, a man of such commanding presence and ringing eloquence that his people called him, not irreverently, "Ol Hi Torrity." When he was the sole Negro in a school of middle-class whites on Long Island, he was already dreaming of becoming a missionary to Liberia—he was searching even then for his lost African heritage—and when the Civil War broke out, he realized, as the coastal Gullahs never did, that this was finally the great War of Liberation. His doctrines of black power—"heart power" he called it—separatism, black capitalism and land redistribution were forged out of the failure of the Port Royal Experiment, launched at Hilton Head to deliver the coastal Negroes out of the shackles of slavery and into the sweetly reasonable world of New England liberalism. And although his part in the experiment is largely unrecorded, he emerged as the spokesman of the bold, new philosophies that were nurtured there, a messiah of the liberated blacks, a man so powerful and magnetic that the mystical Gullahs worshiped him as a reincarnation of Christ while the whites bitterly referred to his regime as "the reign of terror."

Tunis Campbell joined the Port Royal Experiment as an aid to General Rufus Saxton, a vaguely defined post conferred in response to his impassioned pleas to President Lincoln to join the Union Army. Fifty years old, married, and the father of two sons, he was employed by a bakery but his real life's work was the fiery abolitionist speeches he delivered nightly to the New York blacks. Saxton himself was a radical abolitionist. A slender little man with a bristling mustache, a thick Massachusetts accent, and an air of infinite calm, he was that rare sort of military man who, as Arthur Sumner put it, had "a confidence in absolute truth and let the consequences take care of themselves." He had been assigned to take over the loose-knit moral regime of the Experiment missionaries, the nineteenth-century Peace Corps of Harvard, Yale and Andover graduates, Unitarian preachers and Yankee schoolmarms who were teaching the northern primer and the New England virtues to the ten thousand Port Royal area slaves after the defeat of Fort Walker in the Federal amphibious landing at Hilton Head in 1863. Specifically, he was "to make such rules and regulations for the cultivation of the land and for the protection and employment and government of the inhabitants as circumstances seemed to require." Tunis Campbell described his own duties in somewhat loftier terms. He liked to boast that he had been sent to Hilton Head "to organize Civil government, to improve the colored people in the South wherever I could do it, to instruct and elevate the colored race."

At Hilton Head, Campbell had been inflamed by the heady sermons of the Reverend Mansfield French, the chaplain they called the "White Jesus," who promised the "contrabands" not only freedom but massive reparations. "Heart Power" would prevail, he assured them, proclaiming that "God's program involves freedom in the largest sense—free soil, free schools, free ballot boxes, free representation in state and national governments." It was Chaplain French who transformed the reluctant corps of forcibly conscripted blacks into the Gospel Army of hymn-singing crusaders who burned the pretty little town of Darien, ravaged the coastal plantations, and made a slaughterhouse of the Congregationalist church at Midway where the blazing truth of the gospel had first been introduced to the Africans.

In 1864 when the fields set aside for "heads of families of the African race" were abruptly returned to their former owners or sold to northern speculators, Campbell had stood by while Chaplain French urged the blacks to defend their promised land with their hoe handles and Colonel Charles Van Wyck had incited them to "servile insurrection." And after three Federal regiments went berserk, terrorized St. Helena's Island, killed the livestock, robbed and beat the Negro men, and attempted to rape the Negro women, Tunis Campbell had seen enough of northern racism to confirm his belief in separatism.

Separatism had become the golden hope of most of the Hilton Head blacks by the time Sherman arrived in Savannah to present the defeated city to Lincoln as a Christmas gift. Like an avenging messiah, he had come, followed by some 30,000 blacks, chanting in a hallelujah chorus, "No more peck of corn for me, no more pint of salt, no more driver's lash, no more mistress call . . ." Beneath the discreetly shuttered windows of Savannah's manses, his army marched, "swaying to cadence step in unison with martial music," trailed by bands of dancing children, singing "all the rebels gone to hell, now Par Sherman come." The city was locked in a tomblike silence; the wharves which had welcomed the ships of every nation, were deserted, the shops were empty and the women, most of whom were widows now, had no food nor fuel. The city was divided into military districts and the overblown, azalea-splashed squares were crowded with temporary barracks. The carcasses of Sherman's dead horses littered the streets and the old Colonial Cemetery, which had been ransacked for buried silver, was strewn with bleaching skulls. By January, the Savannahians who had raised the emblem "Don't tread on me" over the once impenetrable Fort Pulaski, had voted to submit "to the national authority under the Constitution" and were standing in line "like a ragman's parade" to collect food packets shipped down by New York benevolent societies. When a spectacular fire raged through the city, consuming one hundred buildings including the Confederate arsenal, the vainglorious myth of the Confederacy perished in the holocaust.

General Sherman's Christmas gift to Rufus Saxton and his aide Tunis Campbell was a thousand Freedmen who arrived at St. Helena Village "in a state of misery which would have moved . . . a heart of stone," . . . the "advance (contingent) of a host no less destitute," according to the *National Freedman*. At the Frogmore Plantation that cold, wet, melancholy January, victims of malnutrition and pulmonary disease died at the rate of three or four a day, and Laura Towne, the schoolmarm, reported that "the children are all emaciated to the last degree and have such violent coughs and dysenteries that few survive. It is frightful to see such suffering among children."

Tunis Campbell and the other Negro leaders at Hilton Head had seen enough of southern tyranny and northern racism. They wanted to live by themselves—"there is a prejudice against us in the South that will take years to get over," Garrison Frazier explained to General Sherman at a meeting of eighteen Negro spokesmen—preachers most of them—who assembled at the Green-Meldrim House in January of 1865 to decide the fate of the tattered army of blacks who were starving to death on the docks at Savannah and Hilton Head.

Sherman, in his memoirs, was far less moved by the

historical implications of a black separatist nation within the United States than he was by the humiliating fact that War Secretary Stanton had dismissed him from the meeting to query the Negroes about allegations that the general had tried to prevent the Freedmen from following the Federal army from the interior. "That the great war secretary should have catechized Negroes concerning the character of a general who had commanded a hundred thousand men in battle, had captured cities, conducted sixty-five thousand men successfully across four hundred miles of hostile territory and has just brought tens of thousands of Freedmen to a place of security," he fumed in his journal.

But Garrison's statement had its impact; four days later Sherman issued Headquarters Order Number 15 establishing a Black Separatist empire "from the islands from Charleston South, the abandoned rice fields along the rivers for 30 miles back from the sea and the county bordering on the St. Johns River, Florida.

". . . on the islands and in the settlements hereafter to be established, no white persons whatever, unless military officers and soldiers detached for duty, will be permitted to reside; and the sale and exclusive management of affairs will be left to the freed people themselves, subject only to the United States military and Acts of Congress." Excluding property rights established through the Direct Tax Law, the Negroes could assume tracts not exceeding forty acres, tracts to which they were given "possessory" titles, their occupation protected until "such time as they can protect themselves" or until "Congress shall regulate their title."

As Inspector of Settlement and Plantations, charged with the massive colonizing program, General Rufus Saxton explained the field order to hundreds of Freedmen at a rousing meeting at the Second African Baptist Church. While the blacks intoned their impassioned litany—"Amen," "Hallelujah," and "God bless General Sherman,"—he cautioned them, "In selecting your lands, be sure to get such as were owned by men who have taken up arms against the government or aided the rebellion and who have abandoned their plantations agreeable to General Sherman's order." And Chaplain French assured them, "Your freedom is the gift of God. The President has proclaimed it, and the brave men of General Sherman's army have brought it to you."

When Sherman's field order was reinforced by the establishment of the Freedmen's Bureau, Saxton appointed his aide, Tunis Campbell, "governor of the islands of St. Catherine's, Sapelo and other islands as far as I could reach anywhere within thirty miles," a political domain, enhanced by his spiritual domain, as a missionary of the Zion Methodist Episcopal Church, "over all the provinces of Georgia and Florida." The headquarters of the new government was the home once owned by Button Gwinnett on St. Catherine's Island.

Here came Campbell's people, the hundreds of Negroes living in temporary encampments on the docks at Hilton Head and Savannah whose resettlement was described by William Gannett: "One half of the number had to be helped up the plank, they would drop half way from weakness. Four men only were strong enough to carry up those who could not lift a limb. Long, bony and still, they lay along the docks, the flies swarming around them, as if they lit upon the dead. The silence of four was that of death and before I had them all landed, the four were six. And yet their case has been that of thousands."

Campbell, in his high beaver hat and gold-rimmed spectacles, received them regally as the spiritual heir of Mary Musgrove, the starkly beautiful half-breed princess who had served as interpreter to General Oglethorpe before she turned on the British and marched into Savannah at the head of a band of Creeks to reclaim her empire in a gesture so flamboyant and heroic that the Crown finally deeded three of the coastal islands to her people. Noted the Macon *Telegraph*: "Campbell, that first class buccaneer and filibuster has taken over the governorship of St. Catherine's asserting his authority as the rightful successor of the ancient queen of St. Catherine's in the days of Tomochichi." Wedded to separatism, wedded to black power, he wrote a constitution which was sent to President Lincoln, organized a cabinet, a senate of eight men, a house of twenty representatives, and a supreme court presided over by a chief justice from the Congo whose first act was a law forbidding any white person to set foot on the island, a law reinforced by Campbell's army of 275 men.

Delivered by their Moses into a promised land of teeming forests, dazzling beaches and still fallow fields, the Freedmen gathered in the winter of 1866 at the bidding of Tunis Campbell, to "invoke divine aid and return thanks for His great mercy in delivering us from the bond of slavery." There were then 625 Freedmen on St. Catherine's Island, some 250 of them enrolled in two schools whose faculty included two northern schoolteachers recruited at Campbell's own expense. His work in education won him the vice presidency of the Educational Convention of Freedmen in Georgia held in May 1866. But General Davis Tillson, who had taken Saxton's post in the Freedmen's Bureau, was beginning to refer to Campbell as "a person of great plausibility and remarkable cunning." He noted that Campbell was timbering St. Catherine's; selling the lumber to passing steamers and pocketing most of the money. Also, he had appropriated the best lands, leaving the Freedmen to till a scant 400 acres on the south end of the island, and exist on wild game, fish, and the rations brought in regularly by Yankee gun boats.

Separatism was to be another snare, another delusion. Within two years, St. Catherine's was sold to northern speculators who had already bought up large tracts of the lowlands. Campbell's little army, trying to stave off the invaders, the carpet bag capitalists, finally surrendered to a detachment of Federal troops under General Collins. The empire was gone. "The schools which I had established on the islands were broken up and the people driven off," Campbell wrote bitterly, in his spare, incoherent account of his sufferings in Georgia. Fearing for his life, he journeyed to Augusta to ask General Tillson's protection to resume his spiritual labors as "missionary for the states of Georgia and Florida," then returned to the islands in a sailboat to recruit his scattered people. Their Moses was to deliver them to yet another promised land, a Belleville plantation he had leased from a Union sympathizer named Hopkins. He transported them to the mainland in a lumbering flatboat, daring a blinding rainstorm, only to find that his new domain was "almost worthless for everything was burned up during the war on their place," burned, he neglected to add, by the black Gospel Army under the white Colonel Montgomery.

After a year in exile, Campbell returned to power, this time firmly entrenched in the ballot of a newly enfranchised people. Under the Reconstruction Act of Congress he was appointed registrar for the Second Senatorial District of

Georgia, and promptly registered almost 500 black voters. The whites were disqualified unless they could take an oath that they had not voluntarily taken up arms against the United States Government. Only two white men voted in the election which swept Campbell into office as state senator from the second district and justice of the peace, and a member of the constitutional convention. The press, who labeled him "the old tycoon," commented acidly: "the famous autocrat of St. Catherine's Island aspires to leadership and is perfectly confident of his entire competency to make the Constitution and then administer it."

Campbell moved triumphantly into Darien, the county seat of McIntosh County, and bought a house and several building lots in that devastated little community. Only five buildings had been spared by the Gospel Army who set a torch to the town in 1863; the plantations in the outlying areas had been burned, and the fields were ravaged. The county had sent three full companies to fight for the Confederacy; only fifty men returned, most of them crippled by battle wounds, disease or starvation. The blacks outnumbered the whites by four to one. "The old aristocratic society has been replaced by the most ignorant democracy that mankind ever saw invested with the functions of government," wrote Frances Butler when she returned to Butler's Island, the plantation outside Darien where her mother, Fanny Kemble, had written her bitter diatribe against slavery.

"The country was absolutely swept," she said. "Not a chicken, not an egg was left and for weeks I lived on hominy, rice and fish." In the overseer's shack, where her mother had once served the noted Butler wines and read Shakespeare to the less "barbarous" of the Darien aristocrats, she slept on the bare floor beside a shattered window and kept house for her father, Pierce Butler, beneath a leaky roof, "holding up an umbrella with one hand and stirring with the other."

The Butler slaves, whose abusive treatment Miss Kemble had documented so vividly, came straggling back from the interior to take up their hoes again. "No Missus, we belong to you. We be yours as long as you like," they vowed. Patiently she introduced them to the wage system, which they eyed with suspicion, hired a young Negro teacher from a Philadelphia theological seminary to start a school for the children, and cared for the sick and the aged—stolid old couples like Uncle John and Maum Peggy who came up from St. Simons with a sack of six silver half-dollars received from a Yankee captain for the sale of a Butler chicken during the second year of the war.

While she struggled to establish a new yeomanry, her friends on the neighboring plantations were paralyzed with grief. "Conquered, ruined and disheartened," she described them. "You hear no bitterness toward the North. They are too sad to be bitter. Their grief is overwhelming. The women live in the past and the men only in the daily present, trying in a listless sort of way to repair their ruined fortunes."

Their former slaves were on fire with the heady promises of Tunis Campbell who, courting their vote, "set them against their old masters, filled their minds with false hopes and pandered to their worst passions." His spiritual powers as Methodist overlord of the region gave a messianic dimension to his political offices. The whites were terrified of his capricious use of the law. They were jailed without trial on the slightest provocation—one man for filing a report of a robbery—while on Miss Butler's plantation a known murderer went free because the overseer was afraid to report his crime to the justice of the peace. "The Negroes," she wrote in 1869, "seemed to reach the climax of lawless independence and I never slept without a loaded pistol under my bed."

Campbell also reigned as a labor dictator who, by a nod, ruled whether or not the blacks signed labor contracts with the whites. According to Campbell, many of the contracts "were purposely made to cheat the freedmen out of their labor," and he liked to tell his northern liberal supporters that the blacks who refused to sign were sometimes waylaid and beaten. But if the whites did occasionally resort to force, they were impotent enough to propose offering him a heavy bribe "to use his influence over our Negroes to make them work for us," as Miss Butler put it. She blocked the move, with a bristling statement on the folly of making deals with the devil.

In Atlanta, Campbell, the senator, was proving to be an eloquent and often effective spokesman for black power, black capitalism and for the mute and wretched Freedmen. He was a man of destiny, fighting for the black man at a critical moment in history, fighting a solitary battle in a territory so hostile he swore that when he addressed the Senate, he could hear the ominous click of rifles in the gallery. And the prophetic message he brought like a blazing tablet from the mountain top was chronicled by a press which ridiculed him as an "insolent ape" or dismissed him as an "aged rabbit"—an Uncle Remus character.

As a member of four standing committees—General Education, Pardons, Penitentiary and the Military—he introduced legislation ranging from a bill to prevent common carriers from discriminating among passengers (he'd promised the voters in McIntosh County they would ride the streetcars with the whites) to a permit to incorporate the Georgia Steam Navigation Company—his own venture in Black Capitalism that would transport the Freedmen from his Belleville Plantation to Darien—the town whose charter he wanted declared "inoperative and void." He introduced a resolution assuring that "the stars and bars shall float secure over every part of American soil" and eloquently opposed a resolution which denied there was violence in Georgia. And journeying to Washington, he managed to secure passage of a Ku Klux Klan act after testifying before a congressional committee that innumerable attempts had been made to assassinate him in McIntosh County—an allegation that was never substantiated.

His bitterest battle was fought over the expulsion of a fellow black, Savannah's Senator Aaron Bradley whom the Democrats had found guilty of a felony (rape), a preliminary move to unseat the three Negro senators on grounds that the constitutional right to vote did not imply the right to hold office. The historic consequences of this battle rested heavily on him. Dropping his usual aplomb, he proclaimed from the Senate floor that Bradley must be seated to set a precedent "from the Rocky Mountains to the Rio Grande . . . and extending to time immemorial into the future." He argued with the preacher's impassioned rhetoric until all his peers had left the chamber, "completely disgusted with the Black Ape's insolence," the press reported. When the vote was taken, the vote that unseated not only Bradley but Tunis Campbell, the "old tycoon" went to Washington to appeal to liberal politicians like Senator Charles Sumner, and by January 1870 he was back in the Senate under the protection of a Special Reconstruction Act passed by Congress on December 22, 1869.

But he lost the key battle, the battle against the bill which placed the city of Darien under the jurisdiction of a seven-member McIntosh County Board of Commissioners, a board charged with the same criminal jurisdiction which he wielded singlehandedly as justice of the peace. When the bill passed, Campbell, incoherent with rage, threatened to call on President Grant to send troops to oppose the commission and vowed that the Darien Freedmen would take up arms against them.

He was then at the height of his powers as justice of the peace. Darien had become the black capital of the Georgia coast—the only white man who remained, outside of the Federal troops, was the doctor who sat, lost in the past, in a little cracker box of an office which reminded an English visitor of a Punch and Judy show perched on the bluff. The wharves, noted this visitor, the Episcopal rector who was later to marry Miss Butler, were crowded with "as demoralized a group of negroes as I ever saw." A reporter observed that "Darien is getting to be a regular nest of Negro brigands who rob and assault white people with perfect immunity owing to the fact that all the officials are negroes, chief among whom is that old scoundrel, Tunis Campbell, who ought to be in the penitentiary." The county was terrorized by a black Ku Klux Klan, and by Campbell's own informal army of 150 blacks whom he maintained by exacting a dollar a year from the McIntosh County Negroes. In desperation, the coastal whites, who had bridled at being a subject people under military jurisdiction, petitioned Lieutenant James H. Bradley of the U. S. Infantry, to keep the Federal troops in Darien. "What wonder," he said, "with such a cloud threatening anarchy and ruin." He in turn reported to the assistant adjutant general of the Department of the South that Campbell had become a menace to law and order by telling people "they had a perfect right to judge of the propriety and justice of any law and if they or he believed it to be oppressive and unjust, it was their sacred duty to resist it in any manner and at all hazards."

Now that Darien's shipping industry was coming back, Campbell's reign had assumed international proportions. The once great port, abandoned during the war, teemed with brigs and schooners flying the flags of Great Britain, Germany, Norway, Sweden, Italy, France, Portugal, and Russia. Campbell regarded himself as "protector" of their Negro crewmen —the blacks who loaded the fine yellow pine shipped down the Altamaha River from the great forests of the interior.

When Captain John Irvine swore out a warrant against five crewmen who had tried to seize control of his bark *Grace* on the rough voyage from England, Campbell confiscated his ship and had him arrested without warrant— "dragged along the streets like a dog by the collar," said Irvine, who was jailed, charged with court costs and the back wages of his mutineers.

Irvine finally appealed to the U. S. Commissioner, Henry C. Wayne, in Savannah, who brought Campbell to trial, ironically for violation of his own Ku Klux Klan act. But the pressure from the Washington liberals was too strong. Campbell was released after a series of legal proceedings "irregular and informal to an extent . . . I have never seen exceeded," said one Savannah editor. "The U. S. Government cannot suffer it to pass unpunished without incurring . . . the disrespect of every other nation in the world." And the Democrats, their deep prejudices finally and irrevocably confirmed, declared in print, "the Negro is not only unfit or incompetent to hold office, but actually dangerous, a creator of trouble and a promoter of strife." But Campbell returned triumphantly to Darien, assuring his awed followers that "he was a champion of his race, that he would do in the future as he had done in the past and take the consequences."

He had confiscated four vessels, provoking at least one damage suit against the U. S. Government, before a white justice of the peace in the area felt bold enough to issue a warrant for his arrest. But his following was too powerful. When he was brought in for a hearing, 300 armed blacks surrounded the courthouse and Campbell was freed after he dispersed them, proclaiming with a wave of his hand, "not yet, not yet, this is not the time."

They did finally arrest him in June 1872 on a bench warrant issued by the judge of the Fulton Superior Court for—of all his flagrant abuse of the law—the crime of having joined in holy matrimony a Negro man and a white woman. But he was released on bail; the Darien jail was not strong enough to hold Tunis Campbell.

Out on bond, he was campaigning for a seat in the House of Representatives against John E. Bryant, the Yankee carpetbagger who headed the notorious Custom House ring. The two locked horns at a mass meeting in Savannah. "Calm and serene, like some Egyptian king of old, Tunis Sr. sat while the torrents of vituperation and abuse were poured out upon his devoted head," reported the Darien *Timber Gazette*. When Campbell's time came, "the great tycoon arose, and shook himself for battle," and exposed the "rascalations of the Custom House gang" so eloquently that his followers had to be forcibly restrained from lynching Bryant. But the "old tycoon" had at least one detractor, the Negro Crawford, who maintained "there are some of us, though rice field darkies, he cannot fool. . . . he has as much cheek as a brass monkey and a conscience like Indian rubber." Campbell won the election, but lost it, after a recount, to his Democratic opponent, A. S. Barnwell.

In the interim, a Committee on Privileges and Elections had specifically charged him with flagrant malpractice in his office as justice of the peace by inciting an "insurrectionary spirit" among the people of his district, "advising them to resist a public law of the state with the bayonet." Appended to the committee report was a poignant statement in defense of Campbell, signed by the labored marks of 100 Negroes, declaring that he was "a regular preacher and member of the conference and he told the colored people how to behave and how to live peaceably among themselves." Retorted Alonzo Guyton, the Black Deputy Sheriff, "(whatever) he tells his colored hearers is the law to them, even to putting a man to death."

In 1875, with a half-dozen injunctions pending against him, Campbell met his nemesis in Judge Henry B. Tompkins, an Alabama-born Confederate veteran who, backed by the new Board of Commissioners, managed to lift Darien in a scant year "from a state of anarchy and depression to the healthy plane of prosperity and order," according to the *Timber Gazette*.

One of his first moves was to convict Campbell of false imprisonment of a white man and sentence him to a year in the penitentiary. Eschewing the Darien jail, Tompkins dispatched his prisoner to Savannah; his people followed the train, chanting and weeping as they made the sixty-mile odyssey through the dusty pine barrens. Campbell, "the very picture of sickness and exhaustion," was finally brought before Judge John L. Hopkins of the Fulton County Superior Court, who granted a continuance of the case until Campbell's lawyers could make proper application for bond. Months later, out on bail, the "old tycoon" returned to Darien, only to be indicted for "false imprisonment under color of his office" by a racially integrated grand jury. This time Judge Tompkins allowed his bill of exceptions and freed him on $2000 bail, responding perhaps to pleas like that of Senator H. W. Mattox of Liberty County, a political enemy of the "old tycoon" who introduced a resolution in the Senate requesting the governor to extend executive clemency to Campbell because of "his feeble health and old age."

Campbell, still abusing his power, was soon indicted again on the same charge. His trial was attended by a mob of blacks and a few whites, most of them with pistols hidden in their boot tops. When Campbell failed to give bond and was sentenced to the penitentiary, the mob surrounded their Moses and his captors and held them in the basement of the courthouse. The sheriff managed to get word to Judge Tompkins that he was surrounded by a "boistrous crowd and many threats have been made." When the judge arrived at the courthouse to dispel the mob, they opened fire on Campbell's captors, wounding three of them. Finally a posse was dispatched to quell the riot. All night, while the "old tycoon" was held under heavy guard in the courthouse, hordes of blacks hovered ominously in the square and rifle shots pierced the soft, overblown southern night.

At dawn, Campbell was removed to a makeshift jail on the waterfront. On the second floor of the building armed men stood guard at the windows while the Negroes, sullen and defiant, milled about the wharves, waiting for the *Lizzie Baker*, the steamer that would take the "old tycoon" to Savannah.

When the *Lizzie* docked, three men crossed the docks with Tunis Campbell, an old man now, stooped and defeated, his gold-rimmed spectacles a poignant reminder of his lost glory. The crowd was ominously still as Campbell's footsteps reverberated on the weathered boards. When he mounted the gangway, an ancient, aggrieved black woman threw up her arms and sang, "Goodbye Mas Jesus, Goodbye." As the *Lizzie Baker* steamed out of the harbor, a mighty chorus of African voices took up the mournful chant, "Goodbye Mas Jesus, goodbye."

While Campbell's lawyers took his case to the Supreme Court, the "old tycoon" languished in the Savannah jail, ordering his meals from a hotel and writing dispatches for the northern press on southern atrocities. The Buffalo *Express* quoted him as saying "hundreds have been killed in cold blood in their homes and in the woods." On January 5, 1876, his long battle lost, he boarded the train for Milledgeville under penitentiary guard. Said the Savannah *Morning News:* "It is to be hoped that when he returns to the scene of his villainous exploits that he will have acquired some degree of sense and wisdom." But in the city's *Colored Tribune*, a "weeper for poor Campbell" wrote: "Church people say there is a God.

Well, if there is, if He don't send something upon this state after this He owes an explanation."

Under a new law which allowed the lease of convicts from one to five years, Campbell was leased to T. J. Smith, a Washington County farmer who, impressed by the "old tycoon's" awesome presence, removed his leg chains, fed him from his own table, put him in charge of his gristmill and arranged for him to preach to the other convicts on Sundays. Campbell admitted later that he had been well treated, but he added that Smith's farm was "a weird hole of barbarism" where at least four men had been whipped to death. On January 6, 1877, he was released by Smith who requested that his civil rights be fully restored and testified that he had "never handled a more faithful prisoner."

The "old tycoon," now a martyr of radical reconstruction, scarred by the shackles of a Georgia chain gang, had no intention of remaining in Georgia. He hurried to Washington to recount the epic of his injustices to President Hayes and Morrison Waite, Chief Justice of the Supreme Court. From the pulpit of Washington's John Wesley Church, he thundered that in Georgia the Negro's lot was worse in freedom than it had been in slavery. Negro ministers were jailed "for merely preaching the gospel" and Georgia had become "the empire state of rascality in the South." And he penned a bitter, stirring account of his martyrdom, "The Sufferings of Tunis G. Campbell and his family in Georgia." It omitted any mention of his confiscation of foreign vessels or any of the other legitimate charges against him. It did make a strong case against capitalism— ". . . I ask the laboring man and woman of this nation, How long will it be before you will have no rights that the capitalist or property holder is bound to respect?" And it ended with a heart-wrenching account of his wife's agonized and frustrated efforts to obtain bail for him, an account that had the unmistakable ring of truth. It was enough to confirm the worst suspicions of the northern liberals, for whom he had become a symbol of the betrayal of the abolitionist dreams, of all the high hopes of the ill fated Port Royal Experiment. One of them, Mary Shadd Carey, voiced their sentiments in a poem she wrote as a foreword to "the old tycoon's" book.

And if the gory path
Of Southern empire o'er the bondsman lay
Beneath them lies an early tomb
Low out of thought and sight
Tis but the coming doom
Of those whom God made black instead of white.
"Peace" is our watchword now
At any, every cost or price
Before it honor, trust and country bow
The black must turn to white or die! The last device.

8

St. Simons

LIT BY THE SUN

> 'Tis here thou canst unhand thy heart
> And breathe it free, and breathe it free. . . .

Sidney Lanier found neither health nor wealth when he visited St. Simons Island as an impoverished poet suffering from tuberculosis. But in the awesome silence of the marshes, the cathedrals of live oak, the "sea-liberty" of the island and the strange golden light that gilds the low country, he did find that incandescent sense of infinity which illumines his last poem, *Sunrise*. When he died in Baltimore in 1880, his friends inscribed on his tombstone the blazing sum of his experience among the Marshes of Glynn—"I am lit with the sun."

The liberating effects of the St. Simons landscape have

struck visitors since Jean Ribaut landed there to bargain for sassafras with the Indians in 1562 and described the region as "the fairest, fruitfullest and pleasantest of all the world." Today, the harassed executives who drive in every weekend from Jacksonville and Atlanta are apt to confide similar sentiments to affable Don Everett of the Sailfish Motel. "You know, when I crossed the causeway, something happened," they will say, inarticulate in the face of a quickening joy lost years ago in the board room and the executive suite.

Georgia's largest sea island was considered "our future Eden . . . in the most delightful country of the universe," by Sir Robert Montgomery who in 1717 included it in the ill-starred real estate venture which he called the "Margravate of Azilia," a vast network of feudal baronies along the Georgia coast. France, Spain, and England all laid claim to it before the Battle of Bloody Marsh which reddened the earth with the blood of a hundred Spanish dead and determined English domain on the continent of North America in 1742. Today it is still an embattled island, torn between the industrialists who have sullied the air with a pulp mill, the developers, who are rapidly filling in the lowlands for posh housing developments, and the conservationists, who believe the expansiveness of the salt marsh is a palpable necessity of the human heart.

The landscape is changing with inexorable swiftness and much has been lost. A schoolhouse now stands on the site of the Franciscan mission, built by the Indians who, a generation later, slaughtered the gentle monks at their morning prayers in the bloody coastal insurrection of 1597. The sanctuary was later stripped of its silver bells by the pirate Agramonte, who preyed on the coast from his lair at Turtle

16. Old estate at Jekyll

17. Skull at Cumberland

18. Wild horses roam
Cumberland Island

19. Tamed buzzard on Cumberland

Island off the coast of Cuba. The great plantations like
Kelvin Grove now lend their stately names to housing developments; nothing remains of its role in the golden era of
Sea Island cotton but a few notations in a yellowed plantation book—a record of twenty-eight bales of cotton sent to
market, an offer to sell, and a penciled obituary to a slave
whom they called Aunt Tyra—"What she did for the suffering
and afflicted of her own race will remain as a monument to
her for decades to come."

The slave quarters where frizzled chickens once scratched
for conjure bags is now an antique shop. And on the beach
where Fanny Kemble loved to listen to "the measured pulse
of the Atlantic" the little unpainted houses strewn over the
dunes during the Depression are being replaced by town
houses and fine estates with blooming patios. One hears crisp
Canadian accents among the soft Georgia drawls in the bar
of the King and Prince. The storied old hotel, with its
lavish, lingering Sunday breakfasts of grits and sausage and
its rousing "slavey time" shouts, is fast becoming the in-place
for northern tourists wending their way home from Florida.

New Saint Clair, once the plantation home of James Gould,
is now Sea Palms, a burgeoning, ultra-modern settlement of
motel units, apartments, condominiums, fine brick and glass
homes, a clubhouse, swimming pool, and tennis courts, all
ranged around an eighteen-hole championship golf course of
Tifton Bermuda grass designed by golf architect George
Cobb. Islanders love the Sunday buffets and golf lunches at
Sea Palms. This is their club, and the gatherings before the
crested fireplace in the dining room are reminiscent of the
Saint Clair Club of the 1820s, when the coastal planters
gathered to feast on shrimp pies and shelled crab, to toast

President Monroe, sing songs like "A Valiant Soldier I Dare to Name," and seal their roistering comradery by joining hands for a chorus of "Auld Lang Syne."

Today, at Gascoigne Bluff, guests of the Sea Island Yacht Club dine by candlelight on deviled crab while they follow the course of long, sleek yachts from Newport down the Inland Waterway. Ships from all over the world docked here when the Dodge Meigs Lumber Company operated its flourishing sawmills in the 1870s. Stevedore crews under Henry Armstrong rolled ballast to chanteys like "Hanging Johnny" and "Santy Anna," loading their wheelbarrows to "Annibelle, Hunh! Don't Weep, Hunh!", returning from the river front in a weary chain chanting,

> One a dese mornins, it won't be long
> My soul be at res'
> You a'ks fo' me and I'll be gone
> My soul be at res'. . . .

Many of the old landmarks are gone, but many still remain, thanks largely to the vigilance of Alfred Jones, a Pennsylvania Quaker who took the reins of the Sea Island Company during the Depression and has labored tirelessly to preserve not only the landscape but the unique history of St. Simons.

Fort Frederica National Monument is a tribute to his efforts. Today one can see the mounted turrets that staved off the Spanish invasion of 1742, and the neatly marked squares that identify the commerce of the dead town—the tavern, the apothecary shop, the baker, the carpenter and brick layer, the blacksmith, miller, accountant, surveyor, tithingman, magistrate, and doctor. In the bearded oak forest, where holly and cassina flare amid the mysterious silken glooms, one has a humbling sense of the wildness of this island when Oglethorpe landed here with thirty English tradesmen in 1736 and "traced out a Fort. . . . by cutting up the turf," a fort which was to be the major defense on the Southern frontier of the colonies and a pivot for warfare against the Spanish in southern Florida.

These "citizen soldiers" held the fort until the arrival of three companies of troops from Gibraltar in 1738. Said Oglethorpe of their courage and commitment: "Their presence bridles the Spaniards in America and covers the English Frontiers. The poor people that are here have been so harassed by their threats and so constantly under arms that they have not been able to make that Provision for their subsistence which was necessary though it was far from want of Industry in them . . . It is the vigilance and courage of the Militia that prevented the Spaniards from being Masters of this Province as well as Carolina."

By 1740, the little earthwork bastion had been converted into a "pretty strong fort of tabby which has several 18 pounders mounted in its Front and commands the River both upwards and downwards; and is surrounded by a quadrangular Rampart, with four bastions of Earth, well stockaded and turfed, and a palisaded Ditch . . . On the Rampart are mounted a considerable Quantity of Ordnance of several sizes," so the general described it.

The only real test of the fort came in July 1742, after the battle of Bloody Marsh, when three Spanish galleys converged on the fort. Oglethorpe lined the river banks with musketry and quickly disabled the invaders. War with Spain ended in 1748, and a year later the regiment was disbursed and the twenty cannon were dismounted. When naturalist William Bartram visited Frederica in 1774, he reported, "the fortress was regular and beautiful and was the largest, most regular and perhaps most costly of any in North America of British construction; it is now in ruins, yet occupied by a small garrison." And in 1838, Fanny Kemble viewed the "picturesque groups and masses with the feelings of a European to whom ruins are like a minor chord in music; here they are like a discord. They are not the relic of time, but the result of violence."

The spiritual struggles of the colony are best savored at the two-million-dollar Methodist Conference Center, Epworth-by-the-Sea, erected in 1952 at Gascoigne Bluff as a memorial to John and Charles Wesley, whose memorabilia are carefully preserved in a glass museum, dominated, symbolically, by the painting, "Christ after Chaos."

Historians date the birth of Methodism to the moment when John Wesley's heart was "strangely warmed" in a religious experience at Aldersgate in London in May 1738. But the young minister who came to Georgia on the *Symonds* as a missionary to the Indians and a chaplain to Fort Frederica and left two years later in a long, soul-sick trek on foot from Savannah to Port Royal, found in Georgia the bitter frustration of his stubborn Puritanism that was to deliver him into the larger world of compassionate love.

On his arrival at Savannah, Wesley, then a thirty-three-year-old clergyman of the Church of England, found his Indian charges "tall, well proportioned men," and praised "the remarkable softness in their spirit and gentleness in their whole behavior." But by December 2, 1737, he was confiding in his *Journal*, "They (Indians) are likewise all, except the

Choctaws, gluttons, drunkards, thieves, dissemblers, liars. They are implacable, unmerciful murderers."

His religiosity was shattered by the impious raillery of the frontiersmen of Frederica; his rigid asceticism almost melted before the charms of fulsome Sophia Hopkey of Savannah, his tight-lipped charity hardened to disgust in the face of the violent attacks of Mrs. Hawkins, wife of Frederica's doctor, who tried to shoot him when he questioned the sincerity of her religious conversion. After preaching at Frederica for twenty days in a last, fevered assault against the vagaries of human nature, he took his final leave of "this unhappy place." On January 26, 1737 he recorded in his *Journal:* "It was not any apprehension of my own danger (though my life had been threatened many times) but an utter despair of doing good there, which made me content with the thought of seeing it no more."

That same year, after he had publicly humiliated the newly married Sophia Hopkey by refusing her communion, he was ordered by the court to leave Georgia, and in December, "sneaked away on a favorable tide after evening prayers." Georgians claim St. Simons as the birthplace of Methodism. And it is possible that the bitter failure of his doctrines in the raw new land led him to his final realization that "he who is born of the Spirit, dwelling in love, dwelleth in God and God in him."

Of the plantation era, little remains but the ruins of John Couper's home at Cannon's Point on the Hampton River. A stately avenue of oaks approaches the tabby ruins, where massive chimneys stand like lonely sentinels among the gnarled and broken olive trees that John Couper planted at the request of Thomas Jefferson. The bay laurel that grew—symbolically he thought—out of the stump of the oak which timbered *Old Ironsides* still flourishes here and mournful, vigilant owls lurk among the date palms which Fanny Kemble once admired.

John Couper, who came to America from Scotland in October of 1775, "for the sake of my native land," he always said, built the house at Cannon's Point after the Revolution. His neighbors, who were to constitute the legendary coastal aristocracy, included Pierce Butler, Thomas Butler King, of Retreat Plantation, the original proponent of the Transcontinental railroad who served as U. S. Commissioner in the organization of the territory of California, and the Wyllys, the loyalist family who fled to the Bahamas during the Revolution and returned to St. Simons in the wake of English abolitionist sentiment to take up residence at the Village, once the home of a colony of German Salzburgers.

Frederica Bremer, visiting Cannon's Point in May of 1831 found its red-haired, blue-eyed master "to be a true representative of the gentleman of the Southern states—a very polite man possessing as much knowledge as any encyclopedia." His successful experiments in long staple cotton, sugar cane and olive cultivation earned Cannon's Point a reputation as Georgia's second experiment station. But Couper's interests ranged far beyond agriculture. Sir Charles Lyell was delighted to find in his library such rare books as Audubon's *Birds* and a first edition of Catherwood's *Antiquities of Central America*. In 1776 he was a member of the state legislature and in 1798 represented Glynn County in the Constitutional Convention. His practical and enlightened views on education were adopted by most of the coastal planters. Of his carefree eleven-year-old son William, he wrote: "Next year shall send him to an academy at Northhampton and when he has laid in a sufficient amount of Yankee cunning, I shall send him to Berlin to unlearn roguery and gain honor. At about 24 he may return home to plant cow-peas and pumpkins and eat fat meat as his father has done."

His hospitality was legendary. Guests frequently came and stayed on for years, enjoying the cuisine of his Negro chef, Sans Foix, whose recipe for boned turkey was such a closely guarded secret that the dish was prepared behind a screen. When Aaron Burr was staying alone at Hampton Point after his duel with Alexander Hamilton, Couper sent him "an assortment of French wines, claret and sauternes, all excellent," he wrote his daughter Theodosia. "Also an orange shrub, a delicious punch and Madame Couper added sweet meats and pickles sufficient to last at least twelve months."

Travelers from all over the world were welcomed there. The Honorable Amelia Murray, who stopped at St. Simons on her long journey from Canada to Cuba, wrote of Mr. Couper's estate: "There are from three to 400 Negroes on this estate. Mr. and Mrs. Couper have no white servants; their family consists of six sons and two daughters. I should not like to inhabit a lonely part of Ireland, or even Scotland, surrounded only by 300 Celts. I believe there is not a soldier or policeman nearer than Savannah, a distance of 60 (sic) miles. Surely this speaks volumes for the contentment of the slave population . . ."

Even Fanny Kemble, who scorned the coastal aristocrats as "idle, arrogant, ignorant, dissolute and ferocious . . ." admired the "kind, good humor" of Mr. Couper, found his nursery and kitchen garden "a real refreshment to my spirit," and wrote of his slaves that "he had evidently bestowed much humane and benevolent pains upon endeavors to better their condition."

Bitterly she compared him to Pierce Butler in her *Journal:* "the Scotch tendency of the one to turn everything to good account, the Irish propensity of the other to leave everything in ruins, to disorder and neglect . . . the one made a splendid fortune and spent it in Philadelphia. . . . the other has resided here on his estate, ameliorating the condition of his slaves and his property, a benefactor to the people and the soil alike—a useful and a good existence, an obscure and tranquil one."

Couper's head driver, Old Tom, was "a man of superior intelligence," according to Sir Charles Lyell. The son of a Foulah prince, he had been taken prisoner at the age of fourteen near Timbuktu and was a strict Mohammedan. When Couper's slaves were offered their freedom by Admiral Cockburn in the War of 1812, half of them stayed, heeding Tom's admonition that the British were worse masters than the Americans.

Islanders still talk about the wedding of Caroline Wylly to Couper's son, James Hamilton Couper, a graduate of Yale who studied irrigation and drainage in Holland and pioneered reclamation methods at Hopeton, which the *Southern Agriculturist* praised as "decidedly the best plantation we have ever visited."

In her letters to her mother in December 1827, fourteen-year-old Mary Houston of Marengo Plantation wrote, "Caroline is an almost perfectly beautiful girl. She was very sweet in manner to us both, but I fancied I could see a resignation of expression (as we spoke of her wedding)," not surprising, since the sixteen-year-old bride was about to become the chatelaine of a huge plantation with duties ranging from the management of a burgeoning household to the care of the sick. Mary's letters include detailed descriptions of the wedding dress—"crepe de lisse over a white satin slip"; the elder Wyllys, with their cherished portraits of Wellington and Nelson—"You are forced to recognize that in their hearts they are not Americans but England's loyal subjects"; the demeanor of the groom—"he is so perfectly proper that impropriety gains a charm to those associated with him"; and the bountiful wedding supper of boiled turkey, roast, oyster pies and "syllabub by the 100 glasses."

Highlight of the evening was Johnny, Mr. Couper's Negro choral man—"a marvel, a wonder" who played the bagpipes on the oak-canopied lawn while the Negroes performed gymnastics.

Islanders love to recall how John Couper tried to settle an argument about a new organ at Christ Church by sending Johnny over to play the bagpipes. This was in the days when mail was delivered to the tiny Episcopal chapel for the men to read before the service, when Fanny Kemble shocked both the congregation and her Negro attendants by attending services in a riding habit, and scared the preacher Mr. Bartow who remained "to preach a second sermon to the negroes, on the duty of submission to masters who inter-murder each other," she noted indignantly.

It was here John Couper was buried in 1850, having lived for ninety-one years in what he always considered "the best of all possible worlds."

"His long life was devoted to the duty of rendering himself most acceptable to his Creator by doing the most good to His creatures," says the blurred inscription on his tombstone.

He did not live to see the dissolution of his world, but his son paid a bitter price. Fanny Kemble's daughter, Frances Butler Leigh, was at Butler's Point when he died after lying paralyzed at Hopeton for three years—"the result of grief at the loss of his son, loss of his property and the ruin of all his hopes and prospects."

The steps at Christ Church "were broken down so we had to walk up a plank to get in," she wrote of the funeral. "The roof was fallen in, so that the sun streamed down on our heads, while the seats were all cut up and marked with the names of Northern soldiers, who had been quartered there during the war." As they made their way through the tangled, overgrown yard to the freshly dug grave she swore silently, "Someday justice will be done and the truth shall be heard above the political din of lies."

Christ Church, which dates back to the day Oglethorpe summoned his newly landed troops to evening prayer, is still the heart of St. Simons. The sanctuary, which was almost destroyed during the war, was rebuilt by Anson Green Phelps Dodge as a memorial to his bride Ellen, who died in India on their honeymoon. For almost eighteen years she lay beneath the altar, where he presided as rector until his death in 1898. A stained-glass window pictures him with the son of his second marriage, the young boy to whose memory he established a school after he was killed in a fall from a horse. The Dodges now lie beneath the great pink-lichen-stained oaks at Christ Church cemetery. When Eugenia Price, the noted Chicago author of seventeen best sellers, saw their tombstones on a bleak November morning in 1961, she vowed to tell the brave and tragic story of their lives. Since then she has written two volumes, *Beloved Invader* and *New Moon Rising*, of a projected trilogy on the Dodge family.

The ghost of Christ Church—the ephemeral light that flits between the tombstones—is well known to islanders, who have learned to live amicably with ghosts—the mysterious haunter of the lighthouse, whose footsteps are heard on the spiral staircase at dinnertime, the Ebo Negroes, whose clanking chains can be heard at the landing where they drowned themselves rather than submit to slavery, and Mary the Wanderer who still rides the island's moss-bearded roads astride a white stallion searching for her lover, Raymond Demere of Mulberry Grove, who was drowned over a century ago when his boat capsized in a storm on the Frederica River.

While newcomers are sometimes startled by the specter of Mary on the Demere Road, they find in the ghosts of St. Simons a comforting sense of the continuity of life. They are, at heart, latter-day Protestants, dissenters against the dominant heresies of the twentieth century—conformity, rootlessness, alienation, the corporate rat race and the pursuit of money over truth and joy. They range from writers like Eugenia Price, and Joyce Blackburn, author of the popular Suki series of children's books, who have built a columned tabby home overlooking the marshes, to Mildred Huie, an Albany broadcasting executive who at the Left Bank Gallery has assembled one of the finest assortments of seascapes, wood sculpture, and hand-blown glass on the coast. And they include the young insurance executives who are building second homes at Sea Palms, retired Air Force officers who are opening boutiques in the village, and hard-hitting businessmen embarking on second careers who have found on St. Simons a quality of life they had thought was irrecoverably lost.

With their fierce, wrenching, hard-wrought freedom of the heart, they have attained a profound and speculative reverence for life. And they are jealous guardians of the salt marsh and the sea birds, the splendid silent forests and the torn and shifting beaches that sustain them. Joy, they have found, is as rare as the blue heron—and this is its native habitat.

9

Bessie Jones

SLAVE SONGS AND THE COASTAL SINGERS

In St. Simons' cold, sweet December wind, acorns rained and popped on the tin roof of the Harlem Road Church of God. Bearded oaks, like a company of ancients, brooded in the shadows and cassina bushes studded the sandy churchyard. A fire glowed in the pit; oysters roasted on the iron bedsprings and the saints—Elder Jones and his little congregation of the devout—were relaxing on kitchen chairs, shelling peanuts after a day in the kitchens and yards of St. Simons. The matriarch of the clan, Bessie Jones, bundled in a "northern lady's" castoff coat, her fingers ringed in silver against arthritis, was talking of her grandfather.

"He raised up in Virginia; he been a slave in Virginia. He remember de boat dey bring him in. Dey fool him here. Dey give him sherry wine, money and wine, and fool him over here. Den dey put him under slavery."

The children, bundled in knitted scarves and earmuffs, prodded the oysters with kitchen knives and listened.

"He know his real name; it was Chanki. He never wanted to be called Sampson. He was married twice to the same woman; he married mauma in slavery and then in freedom. I used to mark him there in the field, late in the evening, early in the morning. I used to mark him. He done lay down his life for Jesus; that the only thing he have," she said, and she began to sing:

> I'm go, lay down
> I'm go, I'm go
> Lay down my life for my Lord . . .

The dark, unspeakable heritage of their suffering lay heavy in the silence. An electric light, like a beacon, illumined the little whitewashed church, which the saints had built with their own hands among the kudzu-wreathed cabins in the settlement.

Bessie Jones remembered another song, a song "about how we treated so bad; it come out of our troubles and tribulations."

> Just anyhow, just anyhow
> My Lord Down at the Crown you can Bow
> Just go on living, just anyhow
> Just anyhow, My Lord . . .

They did the ring dances that night, the children pushing, shrieking, and giggling, while Bessie stood in the middle of the circle, brandishing a tambourine, her face majestic in the firelight. They did ring dances like "The Buzzard Lope," and "Who do you love, Roxanne?"; the ring games, "Skip to the Barber Shop," and "Thread the Needle," and the ancient shouts—"Kneebone, I call you Kneebone bend." They did some nameless songs which could only be called morality plays.

"Up in the country in de olden days, our well was open but the white folks' well was covered. In the morning, you go for water and you bail out a snake, you bail out a frog. So they let the white people know how they felt. They don't go hard, they just go easy . . .

Draw me a bucket of water, for my eldest daughter
Frog in de bucket and can't get him out. . . .

And they sang songs with pure African refrains—"oh kum la mumba; oh kum la mumba . . ." chanting the lyrics with delicious abandon, their faces glazed and radiant in the firelight.

The coastal slave songs, the most distinctive music this country has ever produced, are heard only on St. Simons and in the little primitive Baptist churches in McIntosh County. Although they probably originated on the tobacco plantations of Virginia in the early eighteenth century, they were nurtured on the Georgia coast where they flourished in the isolation of the great rice plantations. They had almost vanished when Lydia Parrish, wife of the artist Maxfield Parrish, heard them on St. Simons and organized a singing group called the Plantation Singers. But today, in the tense racial silence of the seventies, they are heard only in those churches where the Negroes still dance the holy dances around the altar and the preachers attain to those unintelligible heights of ecstasy called "trooping." White people heard them only at Mildred Huie's Left Bank Art Gallery or at Alfred Jones's barbecues at Altama until Bessie Jones was "discovered" by the American folklorist Alan Lomax who brought her to New York to perform at a music camp in the Catskills. Since then she has performed at the Newport festivals, appeared in a film and a CBS documentary and given concerts as far afield as Mexico. But these performances offer more prestige than money and Bessie Jones still does day work as a maid and lives in a little cabin in the Harlem Road settlement.

Her healing roots and herbs bloom in tin cans on the window sills and her living room is a cheerful, stout-hearted mixture of make-do. A pink chenille spread hides the tired old sofa, and the walls are decorated with a painting of Christ, a bouquet of pink plastic roses and the seat of a man's trousers—Bessie stuffs her mail in the pockets. A pot of oyster shells simmers continuously on the kitchen stove, a remedy for stomach ailments and low back pain. Sorting through a pillow case bulging with fan letters and mail from people like Harry Belafonte, she recalls the shattering impact of her first invitation to New York.

"When it come, I done prayed to God. I want to live doing something," she said, "something that'll live on. Lord, what must I do?" When the white ladies of St. Simons urged her to accept, she was afraid they were displeased with her housework. Finally, in desperation, she turned to the Scriptures. "I picked the Bible up; I was scared. Teach me to understand, I pray. In reading I got very good understanding. It was the first chapter of Joshua where I opened it, the eighth and ninth verse. It's the only place you find success mentioned," she said, and she picked up the Bible and read:

". . . for this thou shalt make thy way prosperous and

then thou shalt have good success. Have not I commanded thee? Be strong and of good courage; be not affrighted. Neither be thou dismayed, for Jesus thy God is with thee whithersoever thou goest."

Had she opened the Bible instead to the ninth chapter of Joshua, she would have read the verse which southern whites have for generations used to vindicate the practice of slavery: "Now therefore ye are cursed and there shall never fail to be of you bondsmen, both hewers of wood and drawers of water for the house of my God."

In the Catskills, her first brush with integration, she discovered she could delight the children. "They joined onto the things I done. I show 'em. I teach 'em how to clap"—she clapped her strong, silver-ringed fingers together and slapped her palms in the tenor clap, the baritone clap, the bass claps— "and I taught them the Bob Young call. Every country has its own way of doing things, calling chickens, people, hogs. Bob Young was a big, healthy-looked colored man; he get up early in the morning and called peoples up. 'You better raise up, you better raise up and get your 'fore day coffee, Lord, Lord. The Captain is a mean man, the Captain is a mean old man . . .'"

In Williamsburg, she shocked an audience of well-heeled Republicans by telling them her grandfather had been a slave on the Rogers plantation there. "This where he jump over de straw; he and mauma, before dey married, dey jump over de broom. Dey get together and dey jump one foot high," she recalled, adding with a tart sense of outrage. "Den I tell them 'bout de trough. On Sunday dey put in de trough what dey have left from all week. Everything left over dey call 'cush.' Slop is what it was. Dey get together and ringed de trough and dat's how they ate."

Bessie Jones lists her songs in pencil on lined paper in a spiral notebook, carefully classifying them: Ring Games, Ring Dances, Shouts, Work Songs, Shanties, Anthems, Rowing Songs. The academic anglophiles who have studied these unique musical forms usually attribute them to the British airs of the seventeenth century, but their African lineage is unmistakable. They are a product of the musical genius of the early slaves who combined the complicated rhythms of Africa with the more sophisticated melodies of the coastal planters, the unique lyricism of a people who never questioned the essential spirituality of the universe.

"During afternoons of serene weather, men, women, girls and boys are allowed while on deck to unite in African melodies which they always enhance by an extemporaneous tom-tom on the bottom of a tub or tin kettle," noted an African slaver in his journal, one of the few remaining evidences that the Negroes brought their music with them.

The songs had crystallized by 1776 when William Bartram, in his *Travels* wrote of his journey to Darien "the sooty sons of Africa, forgetting their bondage, in chorus sing the virtues and beneficence of their master in songs of their own composition."

Ten years later, Sir Charles Lyell wrote, after a journey down the Hopeton River to the Couper plantation at Cannon's Point, "For many a mile we saw no habitation and the solitude was profound; but our black oarsmen made the woods echo to their song. One of them taking the lead first improvised a verse, paying compliments to his master's family and to a celebrated black beauty in the neighborhood who was compared to a 'red bird.' The other five then joined in the chorus, always repeating the same words. Occasionally they struck up a hymn, in which the most sacred subjects were handled with strange familiarity and which, though nothing irreverent was meant, sounded oddly to our ears, and when following a love ditty, almost profane."

And in her journal, Fanny Kemble commented, with a musician's appreciation: "The high voices all in unison and the admirable time and true accent with which their responses are made always make me wish that some great musical composer could hear these performances. With a very little skillful adaptation and instrumentation, I think one or two barbaric chants and choruses might be evoked from them that would make the fortune of an opera."

The earliest songs on the islands were pure African, and the Negroes who sang them, Gullah Ben and Dublin Scribben, who belonged to the Andersons at Sunbury, are dead now. But Mrs. Parrish has recorded their lyrics—"Rocka Mh Momoba" and "Gu bul-le Al-e."

"Byum-Bye," which originated at the deathbed of a McIntosh County slave, Shisa Shalum, reveals the evolution of the slave song, the haunting combination of fundamentalist Christianity and native mysticism.

> Fa-le-well Shisa Maley
> Fa-le-well en lay vun
> Fa-le-well en lay vun
> An shollen gane en mone
> Shisha har lepentin shu beleven
> Heaven gates are open
> I love Shisha Maley yes Ah do
> Ah anjum biddum ena com
> I love my Shisha yes Ah do
> An anjumbiddum ena cum

The African songs which Bessie learned from her grand-father and discovered again on St. Simons Island are seldom heard in the churches today. "Shout" derives from the Arabic word Saut, which was used among the Mohammedans of West Africa and means to run and walk around the Kaaba or altar. Today, at the Harlem Road Church of God, the saints still dance for the Holy Ghost. On either side of the red felt-covered altar, beneath a primitive painting of Christ, the women rise in a trance from their straight-backed kitchen chairs, dance with infinite grace, alone, their eyes closed, their hands jerking fitfully, as if responding to a rhythm more urgent and compelling than Bessie Jones's ecstatic tambourine.

The saints celebrate religious occasions with shouts like "Ha'k 'E Angels—Day, Day oh—See day's a comin'"—which was first sung in the Praise Houses of Liberty County at dawn on New Year's Day. "Moonlight-Starlight," which originated on St. Simons, is sung at funerals today as it was when Fanny Kemble described the funeral of a slave on Butler's Island: "The coffin was laid on trestles in front of the cooper's cottage and a large assemblage of the people had gathered around, many of the men carrying pinewood torches, the fitful glare of which glanced over the strange assembly. Presently the whole congregation uplifted their voices in a hymn, the first high wailing notes of which, sung all in unison in the midst of these unwonted surroundings—sent a thrill through all my nerves."

Shouts like "Down to the Mire," in which the dancers circle around the supplicant, tapping their heels like drums, recall the ceremonial dances of Africa.

Sister Emma, oh you mus' come down to de mire
Sister Emma, oh you mus' come down to de mire
Jesus been down to de mire
Jesus been down to de mire
Honor Jesus to de mire. . . .

"Knee Bone," in which the shouters symbolically kneel and rise, may well be one of those shouts which Fanny Kemble described as "extraordinarily wild and unaccountable." And "Oh Eve—Where Is Adam?" is a haunting mixture of Old Testament theology and the native African question and response song form. "Oh Eve—Where is Ad-um? Oh Eve—Adum in the garden pinnin leaves," they chant, evoking with their hypnotic gestures all the lost fruits of Paradise.

Music on the coast, as in Africa, grows out of the rhythmic movements of labor—rowing, loading freight, threshing rice. In his *Travels in North America* (*1827–1828*) Captain Basil Hall wrote of hearing slave songs during a canoe trip from Darien to St. Simons. "The oars were pulled by five smart negroes, merry fellows and very happy looking . . . They accompanied their labors by a wild sort of song not very unlike that of the Canadian voyageurs, but still more nearly resembling that of the well-known Bender boatmen of Bombay." In Brunswick, vessels are sometimes loaded to the musical chant of "Sandy Anna" and freight cars at the sugar terminal are shunted for short distances to the singing of "Old Tar River." These work songs are not melodic but rhythmic, short phrases of two or three bars, with a staccato chorus of two or three ejaculatory words.

Befo this time another year
   I may be gone
In some lonesome grave yard
   O Lord how long!
Mind my sister how you walk on the cross
   O Lord how long
Your right foot slip and your soul get los'
   O Lord how long.

And as shrimp boats return to the coastal harbors at dusk, you can hear the crew men chanting,

      Sun is down an I mus go
      Sundown
      Sundown below . . .

Rice hasn't been planted since the lean years after "The War," but you can still see dances at Altama, the dancers, in starched white aprons, going ceremoniously through the ancient ritual of tying up the sheaves and whipping them with "frails." The old-timers hoed rice to the tune of "Way out yonder in that new bright worl'," tied up the sheaves to "Do Lord Remember Me" and whipped it to the chant, "Turn Sinner Turn—Sinner Wouldn't Turn." A short song was often used for the rice dance, the thrashers moving in a circle, chanting, "You know the way an' you wouldn't come home," then hopping on one foot and shouting, "Make a jump for joy!"

These songs are exotic remnants. But at baptisms on the ebb tide at the Frederica River in a ritual that recalls the river-worship at Dahomey, you can still hear the faithful chanting, "If you don' believe ah been redeem; Gawd's go'nah trouble duh watuh/ Follow me down to Jordun stream/ Gawd's go'nah trouble duh watuh. . . ."

The path to faith often follows an agonizing spiritual struggle on the "anxious seat" or the "mourner's bench." In the old days, sinners would wander for hours at night before "coming through," and the saints on Harlem Road still pray fervently for a union with God. From the altar rail, a sister will implore: "Continue to pray for me, those who can get a prayer through."

> My head got wet by the mid'l-night dew
> livin' humble, livin' humble.
> My head got wet by the mid'l-night dew
> Livin' 'umble, livin' 'umble. . . .

Every ritual has its poetry—"drinkin of the wine-wine-wine; drinkin of the wine; O-yes-My Lord; I oughta been to heaven ten thousand years; Drinkin of the wine." Majestic sermon-exhortations have been set to music—"Stop let me tell you bout the Chapter One, When the Lord God's work has jus' begun. . . ." But the most achingly beautiful songs of the coast grew out of the awesome mystery of death. They are sung at "settin' ups," when the mourners gather around the fire, in the presence of the dead, to sip coffee and chant,

> Ferry boat goin to carry us over
> De robe all ready now.
> Ferry boat goin to carry us over
> De robe all ready now

At the graveside, grief approaches ecstasy as the dead approaches the vast, liberating spirtual reaches of Paradise. "U-m-h, u-m-h, I hear a mighty moanin'," they hum with closed lips, slipping into a trance, a mystical dimension of sorrow far beyond the white man's ken.

Y'u're goin to miss me for my prayer
Y'u're going to miss me for my song
Church I know y'u're goin to miss me when I'm gone.

These are coastal songs, but Bessie Jones has added to them the songs she learned from her grandfather in the fields near Dawson, Georgia where, as a child, she swept porches for a dollar a week. Her tambourine then was made of Coca-Cola bottle tops, and her songs were drawn out of the bitter poverty of the pine barrens. "Massa killed a big old duck, give us all the bones to suck . . ."

New coastal songs are being born every day, emerging full blown out of the sunny, bittersweet, sea-stung life on the docks and in the canneries of Brunswick. Listen to Bessie tell the ballad of Robert Johnson, the wood peddler from North Carolina:

"He down here in this county, a raggedy man, standing on the dock, looking across the water. A woman come there, down to the water. He have on overalls, look po, but she like this man. You know, charm for charms. He look up and see 'yes' on her face. He told her he making a living working selling kindling wood. So she joined up with him. Both of them they kind of low in looks. He an old raggedy man, she an old raggedy woman, and they go about selling kindling wood together. She and he bought them a house; they had their dinners of chicken and rice, they bought them a car and the word got around they had been to the root man and had them a rabbit foot. But the rabbit foot come

20. Slave chimney recalls cotton kingdoms on Cumberland

21. Cumberland Island by air

22. Bob Rischarde of Cumberland Island

from working together, it come from love," she says and then she croons:

My name is Robert Johnson, all the way from North Carolina
I am selling kindling wood to get along . . .
Yes I've got the left hind foot of a rabbit
All I got to do is reach out and grab it
Oh how happy I feel
I can eat chicken and I don't have to steal. . . .

When Bessie is with the other singers, with Emma and John David and Henry, songs are born out of the simplest incident. When Henry discovered someone had put whiskey in the water bucket at Newport, "we all act nice, act mannerable, but we make a song about it and dat song done gone down in history. . . . 'Big Bull Ratty Come join the band, Waaa, Waaa, Waaa . . .'"

Songs are frequently born at the Harlem Road Church of God. On Sunday mornings, you'll hear among the old songs their own answer to Christian atheism, "God's Not Dead." You may also hear Bessie preaching, standing in a bare, wooden pew, the sunlight gilding her brave, beautifully etched face.

"Everybody is a bastard child that doesn't know God is his father," she tells the saints. "My grandfather as a slave told his brother, 'I gone learn you, get on your knees, I'm gonna teach you how to pray, Say Our Father; Our Father; Our Father.' Jess say 'no' and get off his knees. 'I'm gonna teach you to pray,' my grandfather say. 'You not gone be like the other negroes.' 'I'm not gone say our Father,' said Jess. 'If we were brothers, massa wouldn't treat me like he do.' But God love all his chillun. He don pick none cause he made 'em all."

Sometimes Bessie Jones draws her sermons from her travels. "I went in the ambassador's house in Mexico and got all bogged up in the rug," she begins. "We sit down in some fine chairs and we served by the great waitresses. I don' know if they colored or not—you can't tell with them Mexicans. It's de prettiest place and the women wear dem robes. Emma say you see dem gowns a yonder, you know dey fine clothes. But I say dere's something better dan dis, dis gone be destroyed. We build dis church, but it gone be destroyed. Only thing stand is the word of God. The Mexicans is day laborers. Dey working people, dey building up dis thing like we done in the South. Jesus say you have the poor with you always. But I know Jesus is in me, He's rich, He's rich in spirit."

Bessie's son, Elder Jones, has a way of chanting his prayers while the saints kneel at the altar, in a trance-like state, a sweet, fevered, mystical union with their Lord.

"Saints whatever you do, let it not be done in strife. As Christians we become children of God. . . ."

Bessie slaps her tambourine, and the saints begin to sing:

> I come over here to stay Lord
> Till I die
> I come over here to live Lord
> Till I die. . . .

"Our lives are an example to the world that they can see Jesus in you. You must be born again, children . . . You must have love one to another," chants Elder Jones.

Following Bessie Jones's unfaltering, deep-throated so-

prano, the saints intone a chorus. Washed by tears and sunlight, their ebony faces are innocent; their bodies sway gently
around the altar rail; they are holding hands. . . .

> We've come this far by faith
> Lean on the Lord,
> Trusting in his holy word
> He never failed us yet. . . .

10

Sea Island

GRANDE DAME OF RESORTDOM

> Wish I wuz Mr. Alfred Jones' son
> Stay in de House and drink good rum. . . .

The soft-spoken Negroes of St. Simons added this refrain to their work chanteys in the bitter days of the Depression when the descendants of the great families were reduced to living in the tabby outhouses of their dwindling plantations and the Washboard Band was singing all night on the beaches for the grudging pennies of former millionaires.

The Negroes were singing not so much of Alfred Jones as of the miracle of Sea Island; they were singing of the Cloister Hotel which he had created, like some improbable pleasure dome, on the forgotten island where the Wyllys and the Coupers once grazed their cattle. The shining palace was built upon the sand. Alfred Jones then had little more than the mortgages and a dream. But the Cloister, with its Mediterranean red-tiled roof, its stained-glass windows and filigreed wrought iron, was real enough—a golden spa where the survivors of the crash still donned black tie for dinner, surveyed the ruins of the stock market from a radiant court-yard and spoofed Roosevelt and the New Deal in a cruel and merry little song which the Negroes still chant at Plantation suppers on the bluff.

People like Herbert Hoover and Calvin Coolidge and Princess Juliana stayed at the hotel, and Eugene O'Neill lived in a walled house on the beach during the crucial gestation period before he wrote *Long Day's Journey Into Night*. Dick Everett, the Cloister's manager, still remembers him, a solitary, striving figure, swimming far out beyond the breakers at dusk.

Today, the Beautiful People go to Hope Sound or Sun Valley in the winter, to the Fairmont in the spring, the St. Regis in October. To hire a Serge Obolensky to lure them to Sea Island, to prevail on Wendy Vanderbilt to give a party would be, one feels, distinctly beneath the Cloister's dignity. For the Cloister is less a hotel than an arbiter of taste, the *grand dame* of resortdom, impervious to the great revolu-tions, the violent changes, and the new barbarism of the seventies. Here and only here, can one be certain that dinner will be served precisely at eight, that gentlemen will don black ties on Thursday evenings, that one's bed covers will be turned down in a perfect V at night, and that finger bowls will be offered at breakfast.

The great upheavals of the twentieth century have wrought only two changes at the Cloister. Among the guests there is

a new breed of bright young men with vague backgrounds—
"in rubber, in Akron"—and lovely wives who do their own
housework and find the Island's Spanish moss vaguely disturbing—"like cobwebs," they will tell you, as if they were
longing for a broom. The most maverick of these achievers
submits humbly to the Cloister's benign paternalism, hurrying
their cocktails against the hotel's rigid dinner hour. With
their coming, some of the old-timers complain, the summer
season has taken on the aura of the Macon Country Club,
but the Cloister, with its unique civilizing properties, manages
to give even the most rough-hewn an air of "to the manor
born."

The new people have come and the Negroes no longer
come to the Cloister to "shout" on Sunday nights. But at
Island cocktail parties, the old-timers will show you how it's
done, going round and round, shuffling and tapping their
heels to the rhythm of a broomstick pounded on the floor.
The plantation owners outlawed drums after the Stono Rebellion of 1739 when the South Carolina slaves, inflamed by
a drum-beat, launched an insurrection in which dozens of
whites and Negroes were killed. "Knee Bone Bend" and
"O Eve Where Is Adam?" and "On the Eagle's Wing"—
the Negroes used to shout them in the austere little cabin
of Mrs. Maxfield Parrish who appreciated, as few white
people ever have, the strangeness and beauty of the shouts
and preserved them in a scholarly book called *Slave Songs of
the Georgia Sea Islands*. Mrs. Margaret Davis Cate brought
the "shouts" to the Cloister after Mrs. Parrish's death, but
when Sea Island's own historian died, the singers drifted away.

Yet at the Cloister, life goes on as usual. The hotel is
almost always full. Three fourths of the guests are returnees

who have come to cherish the Cloister style, the superb service, the traditions—the Yule log at Christmas and the Easter egg rolls—and the infinite attention to detail. They love the morning song of the little yellow birds in the Solarium at breakfast, the walks bordered by paper-white oleanders, the loggia where fountains play among the exotic Chinese red hibiscus. Even the eternal sprinklers on the nine-hole putting green are regarded as symbols of the Cloister's continual vigilance and solicitude.

You'll find the young executives on the Teniko tennis courts or at the Cloister's fine twenty-seven-hole golf course across the causeway at St. Simons. Youngsters love the horse-back rides across the dunes and the older people, merry vagrants of generous pension plans—enjoy bowling and croquet on the impeccable lawns. The perennial honeymooners—a thousand a year—prefer the beach where the surfing is good and the sand sailing is sometimes hair-raising. At lunch everyone gathers at the Beach Club to take the sun around the free-form pool, to sip rum drinks in the bar, and sample the fine buffet—a gourmet's selection of hot shrimp dishes, roasted meats, and seafood salads. Guests dine at little umbrella-top tables on a terrace overlooking blowing sea oats, the long white breakers, and a strip of wild and brilliant beach visited by gulls and jet black grackles.

The timing at the Cloister is precise and unvarying. Cocktails are served in the club-rooms at seven; the bar closes at seven forty-five. Dinner is at eight, an elaborate meal that opens with vichyssoise and closes with Continental cheeses and fruit. Later there is bingo and duplicate bridge, and, on Saturday night, dancing on the terrace to the comfortable tunes from *My Fair Lady*.

On Friday nights the men don Bermuda shorts, the women wool slacks and fine silk blouses and take the jeep train down the beach to the bluff where the Plantation suppers are held. It is like a journey back in time to the clearing in the forest of tortured oaks where the eerie light of *flambeaux* sears the hoary beards of Spanish moss. The vast salt marsh undulates in the fierce dusk and stark white birds flick through the mysterious glooms. While the guests sip gin and tonic at the Cloister's neat little outdoor bar, Simon Bailey presides over steaming pots of shrimp mull and fried trout and hush puppies. "It was twenty years ago we first came here to cook," he recalls, his magnificent black face softened by nostalgia. "It was a Mr. Kennedy from New York—him and me came here with two beers and a pint of whiskey and cooked up a fish. He told his friends about it, about this place, and soon they were coming too and it grew. You know how there're days you have the blues and you can't get out of bed? In twenty years only once I had the blues like that. Five, six, seven o'clock—whatever time Mr. Alfred Jones said, Simon Bailey was there. . . ."

As the guests take their places at the long plank tables, a Negro quartet from St. Simons breaks into the old work chanteys. "One of these days I'm going away, won't be back till judgment day . . ." Their voices rich, monotonous, rhythmic, and despairing, evoke the bitter ghosts of the marshlands—across the sound at Ebo Landing, a group of Ebo Negroes once joined hands and walked into the water, giving themselves to the sea in a mute and hopeless protest against slavery.

The past is far more reassuring in the golden daylight. On the golf course, which was once Retreat Plantation, a mile-long avenue of oaks still stands, a relic of the proud days when the Kings were among the reigning families of the coastland. Here are the tabby ruins of the slave hospital where Mrs. King tended the sick and recorded the inevitable deaths—"My good and faithful servant Hannah after years of suffering expired on the night of 3rd August, 1854 . . . She died resigned, with firm trust in her Redeemer." The Golf Club, originally the Retreat corn barn, was built of tabby by slave labor in the 1840s. In its shadows, cloistered by oaks, is the little graveyard of the slaves. Here lies Neptune Small, who brought the body of his master, young Captain Henry Lord Page King, home from the Battle of Fredericksburg to be buried in the family plot at Christ Church. Near him, in a grave marked by a faded little American flag, lies young Samuel George, killed in Vietnam on May 20, 1967.

The Cloister's carefully marked remnants of the past are indicative of Alfred Jones's concern for the integrity of the coastal islands. Insiders will tell you his stamp is everywhere, from the moss-canopied drives (the Sea Island Company has won the battle of the billboard), to the battlements of Fort Frederica (the restoration was his idea) to the Cloister grounds where two magnificent scarred bells recall the gentle tenure of the Franciscan monks of the seventeenth century. It was Alfred Jones who provided the Cloister with its first historian in residence, Margaret Davis Cate, whose lectures on coastal history are fondly remembered by older guests. Her book, *Early Days of Coastal Georgia* is still a favorite of islanders. Once a guest who carelessly left a copy on her bed was chastized in a scribbled note from the Negro porter who came in to turn down the covers. "Don't leave important things on the bed," he wrote. Mrs. Cate's fierce devotion to the island's heritage has become legendary. Sea Islanders will tell you with ill-disguised relish that after she lost her battle to have indigenous azaleas planted at Fort Frederica, she returned to the park every spring to snip blossoms off the highland plants.

The lectures now are delivered by Dick Everett, who has been with the Cloister since 1934 and who shares Mrs. Cate's almost mystical feeling for the beauty of the islands. Everett can speak with authority of the first owners of Sea Island, the Jekyll Island Club which purchased the property in 1888 under the aegis of a flamboyant Irish-born promoter, James F. O'Shaughnessy. Everett is an historian of the Jekyll Island Club, the group of millionaires who occupied the great homes at Jekyll until the bombing of Pearl Harbor ended their golden sojourn on the island. The Cranes, the Rockefellers, and the J. P. Morgans wintered at Jekyll in a "state of sweet euphoria, marred only by the infirmities of old age," says Everett. "They regarded death not as a cessation, but as a transference from an earthly to a heavenly paradise." At Sea Island, he finds that same "sweet euphoria."

The Sea Island Company was originally formed by Detroit industrialist Howard Coffin, who lived on Sapelo in the pink stucco palace known to newcomers as "the Reynolds' place," to natives as the site of South End Place, the plantation home of Thomas Spalding. Alfred Jones, Coffin's cousin, came to Sapelo as a University of Pennsylvania student to recover from an illness, stayed on to join the Sea Island Company, and pioneered, under Coffin, the development of the island as one of the most ambitious real estate ventures on the Eastern seaboard. In 1928 he took it over, after the

Depression abruptly ended Coffin's dream of a residential community dominated by a yachting basin and polo fields.

Everett regards the Depression as the determining factor in the Cloister's unique character. "The Sea Island Company retrenched from developing property to operating the hotel. It forced the Cloister to cultivate and nurture the personality of a resort. That is the heart of what we have now . . . the intangible atmosphere, the unspoken policy. We cared about people and they cared about us."

As the Depression lifted, the Cloister guests began to build homes on the island, homes whose fine Mediterranean lines and patterned gardens were discreetly dictated by the land-scaping committee of the Sea Island Company. "We were able to build up an almost paternal relationship between the hotel and the homeowners," Everett recalls. "There was an accepted convivality, a personal relationship. There was no one in the houses who could not call us and ask for anything—we would either do it or explain why we couldn't. We still try to instill that spirit in all our working staff, that rapport."

Inevitably, in the shadow of the Cloister, there arose a social kingdom, presided over by a ruling family—the Abreus, who own what is still the most distinguished house on the island—and dominated by at least three *grandes dames*, one of whom receives her guests with a floppy hat clamped on her forehead and a pocketbook dangling from one arm. The old gods prevailed—the hierarchy was based on money, birth, and longevity, and gold-plated WASP credentials were required of all newcomers. "I know of no one on Sea Island who doesn't give a damn. They all give a damn—about the wrong things," says one frequent visitor to the Cloister.

Everett would disagree. The old exclusiveness is giving way to what he describes as "democratic *joie de vivre*. I can remember when people like Mrs. Stratton wouldn't think of accepting an invitation from a stranger unless they had known her mother in college. Today Mrs. Stratton goes everywhere."

Everett's own Beach Club parties reflect the new Sea Island aristocracy—an aristocracy neither of birth nor wealth nor even achievement; an aristocracy of aesthetics. After the first martini, the guests from Philadelphia or New York are likely to confide: "Sea Island is the only place where I can be myself." There is a sensitive response to the moon-washed sea beyond the glass walls, the tangy air and the pale oleanders at the gate. Octogenarians, with the sweet naïveté of children, do a dance called "King of the Road" and retired industrialists gather around the organ to sing hymns like "The Old Rugged Cross" and "Shall We Gather at the River." The air of permanence is so reassuringly pervasive that one feels a definite chill when someone remarks, "I hear the Cloister is advertising for help."

"The Cloister—advertising?"

For a moment the rhythm of the evening skips a beat. The fire flares beneath the lobster pot and sparks fly on a sudden fitful wind.

Dick Everett summons two waiters; the wind dies and the fire subsides. Someone is handing out white linen bibs; the lobster is done, the bar is closing, and in the shadows, a waiter shields the dessert—plump strawberries in brandy and whipped cream.

An aging Republican from Pittsburgh, a perennial guest of the Cloister, remarks, "how good it is to come to the end like this."

11

Jekyll Island

MEMORIES OF THE "MILLIONAIRES' CLUB"

The cannon sounds no more at Jekyll Island. Once it announced the comings and goings of the presidents of the Jekyll Island Club—the millionaires' club whose hat rack bore the names of Astor, Morgan, Carnegie, Pulitzer, and Rockefeller, all told, one sixth of the world's wealth. It was the most exclusive club ever known, one hundred of the world's wealthiest men quartered on an island nine miles long and one mile wide. The only fear any of them knew was the fear of death, and when the cannon failed to shoot, the island Negroes said it presaged the death of a president.

It was the fear of death that brought them to Jekyll Island, then a little-known island off the Georgia coast. Looking for a spa that would be the healthiest place in the world, the robber barons who founded the Jekyll Island Club dispatched two doctors from Johns Hopkins to explore the world for a resort that could offer a mild semi-tropical climate, natural beauty, good water, isolation, and reasonable proximity to Wall Street. The scouts ranged from the Riviera to the southern shores of the Mediterranean and finally recommended the Golden Isles of Georgia in the favored latitude of the Riviera, Cairo, and San Diego.

Today, the island which was once so cloistered that a guest like Winston Churchill was called a stranger, is a Georgia state park, open to everyone. Tourists from every state in the union crowd its motels, its two championship golf courses and the nine-hole course where J. P. Morgan once tipped his caddy a nickel. Visitors are anxiously awaiting the opening of the fresh-water marina, banked by oyster shells, and the motel at the south end of the island is already booked far in advance by youth groups. So many Canadians came down every year that the flag of Canada floats over the island during the winter months and every comer has access to the golf club on the island on which the millionaires took care that "no unwanted foot ever touched" in the sixty-one years of its existence. There is no longer any such thing as an unwanted foot, Horace Caldwell, affable head of the Jekyll Island Authority, will tell you.

In sharp contrast to the new motels, the aquarama for convention meetings and the giant slide for children, stand the old estates. Most of them are sinking into disrepair, empty, echoing mansions whose gargoyles and concrete lions have lost their ferocity, seedy, slightly sinister memorials to another era—what Tallu Fish, the island historian, calls the glamour era. But they are being gradually restored. Most notable now is the Rockefeller cottage, with its stained-glass windows and carved mahogany newel posts and huge bedroom vaults—for "pocket change" the islanders will tell you. This has been restored as a museum for memorabilia of the golden era. The old hotel, where no guest was allowed to stay over two weeks, is open too—in the library, visitors can see the guest book and note the last signature, that of General George S. Patton, who was sent to vacate the island when a German submarine was sighted off Jekyll and the government feared the nation's wealthiest and most powerful men would be kidnaped by the Germans.

But Jekyll history did not begin with the "millionaires' club," though their lingering memory adds a sheen to the island. The local people still delight in their Paupers' Club, a club in which they take the millionaires' names—Astor, Vanderbilt, and Morgan—for the annual Christmas banquet to which they bring their own gourmet dishes.

Jekyll's history began with the Muskogean tribes of the Creek nation whose village was called Ospo. Agrarians, their year revolved around the feast of the First Fire. It opened with the Green Corn Festival in the square of the village Ospo, where trials were held for the year's offenses, and culminated with the ritual of the black drink, in a huge bonfire in which the residue of the old year, from old clothes to garbage, was burned in a great conflagration with ceremonial dances. But the Muskogeans could be cruel—prisoners were tortured until dead in the town square and scalps were taken and used in orgiastic victory dances. It was this cruelty which was to result in a mass Indian massacre of the kindly Franciscan priests who settled among them in the sixteenth century. The missionaries, introducing the practice of monogamy and substituting their own rituals for the Indians' cherished ceremony of the First Fire, soon provoked the Indians to wrath—they wanted no more of Catholic spiritual anarchy, and at a meeting in Darien they vowed to put an end to the Franciscans. All the monks on the Georgia sea islands were slaughtered at the pulpit but one, Father Davila, who was hit by three arrows and enslaved in an island village. Stripped of his clothing, he was made to walk through the village naked and given nothing but leaves to eat. At intervals he served as a target while the boys of the village practiced with bows and arrows. Brutally beaten and incessantly teased, Father Davila remained serene in his faith, a serenity that so angered the Indians that they lashed him to stakes and piled firewood around him, offering him an opportunity to embrace their religion before they burned him alive. When he refused, an Indian woman intervened in his behalf to save her son who was being held at St. Augustine for having participated in the slaying of the village priests. While Father Davila's life hung in the balance, a Spanish scout searching for him along the Georgia coast managed to get a note to him, through an Indian messenger, offering to exchange him for the Indians whom the Spanish were holding as prisoners charged with murder. But even after he was rescued and delivered to St. Augustine, the priest refused to testify against the Indians, saying that it was contrary to the canons of his church.

The martyrdom of Father Davila may have made it possible for the Spanish to continue their spiritual domain over the Indians. During the Easter season of 1606, Bishop Altamirano was dispatched to visit the Georgia islands and confirmed a total of 1652 Indians in Georgia and Florida, but in the end his golden promises of redemption and salvation were betrayed when a group of Indians flocked to St. Augustine to help the Spanish stem a threatened European invasion and were imprisoned and enslaved.

Oglethorpe's victory at Bloody Marsh brought an end to Spanish domination of the coast. Oglethorpe named the island for his friend Sir Joseph Jekyll, and constructed a brewery there to assuage the thirst of his troops before slavery was introduced and the duBignon family from France ushered in the golden era of Sea Island cotton, an era that was to end in a national scandal when the slave ship *Wanderer* landed at the island with the last shipload of slaves ever brought to this country. This was in 1858, almost a half century after the U. S. Government outlawed the slave trade and condemned it as an act of piracy. The ship was owned by W. J. Corrie of New York and Savannah's flamboyant Charles Lamar and flew, ironically, the flag of the New York Yacht Club, though it was built specifically for slave traffic. In 1858 the ship made its first and last voyage to Africa. The crew, using quantities of beads, trinkets and knives, managed to entice 350 Africans on board. Fifty of them died in the hold during the middle passage. Before federal authorities got wind of the *Wanderer*'s mission, all but a hundred of the *Wanderer* slaves who landed on Jekyll had been sold in South Carolina. Years after the Civil War these hapless Freedmen were still yearning for their African homes. In 1904 a Negro named Ward Lee, who still clung to his African name Cilucangy, was futilely circulating a petition to his white friends in Trenton, S.C. His plea: "To the public: Please help me. In 1859 I was brought to this country when I was a child. I cannot say what age

I was then but I have been aroused by the spirit—and I trust it was the spirit of God—on last May. One year ago it was revealed to me to go home back to Africa and I have been praying to know if it was God's will and the more I pray the more it presses on me to go. . . . And now I beg everyone who will please help me. . . . I am bound for my old home if God be with me . . . white or black, yellow or red I am an old African."

The square black kettle used on the *Wanderer* stands on Jekyll now, near the old hotel, and the natives will tell you that when the coastal northeasters blow up, the voices of long dead slaves can be heard howling for their families and for their homelands.

Another company of ghosts, those of the storied millionaires, also haunts the old hotel. This was Jekyll's golden era, and few islands have ever known such a concentration of wealth and power. The Jekyll Island Club was launched with simplicity—in 1887 a rambling clubhouse was built and the island was stocked with English pheasant, deer, and wild game. King Humbert of Italy sent a gift of 300 wild boars to the island. The general atmosphere was informal—clubmen and their wives came without formal dress, the rooms were small, there was a single creaking elevator, and cocktails were served in the evening in a lounge furnished with a huge poker table and a 500-pound leather sofa.

Non-members, regardless of who they were, were considered strangers, and that included Winston Churchill and President McKinley, who visited Jekyll in its heyday. Membership was by inheritance only. Boats approaching the island were screened by offshore guards and the only press ever permitted ashore was charter member Joseph Pulitzer, editor of the St. Louis *Post-Dispatch* and the New York *World* and founder of the Columbia University School of Journalism.

If the club was exclusive, it was not always intimate. Many of its members were often at cross purposes; the islanders still gossip about them at the Paupers' Club. There was J. Pierpont Morgan, who was noted for his timesaving devices. Once tied up in New York traffic, he ordered his chauffeur to drive down the sidewalk, then sat back calmly while the pedestrians scattered in every direction. There was the irascible James Cook Hill who once fired a genial employee because his name was Spittles. Jay Gould, noted for his ruthlessness and his skill at fast dealing, once presented his card to one of the Rothschilds and had it returned promptly with the scrawled message, "Europe is not for sale." And when Pulitzer attacked him in the press, Gould simply replied, "So what, I'm on top, ain't I?"

The simplicity which had marked the club's inception soon degenerated into high-level status seeking, with members vying to see who could own the largest yacht or build the most opulent cottage mansion. Plumbing magnate Richard Crane's house, modeled after a Byzantine palace, had twenty-one bedrooms and seventeen baths, several of them with gold plumbing fixtures, and the house itself was partially furnished with tables and benches from an ancient Italian monastery. Jay Gould's palace, approached by sweeping stairs whose entrance was guarded by two hand-carved Corinthian lions, had a swimming pool just inside the front door. One of the least ornate was the simple and tasteful Rockefeller home which is now being restored to house the Jekyll museum to which Tallu Fish has contributed her extensive memorabilia. None of the cottages contained kitchens as all cooking was done in the enormous kitchen of the hotel by the finest chefs of Delmonico's famous restaurant in New York. The sumptuousness of the cuisine was legendary, and it was not uncommon for dinner to last three hours.

Over the poker tables after dinner, the conversation usually revolved around money and the adroit machinations by which the club members had amassed their fortunes. Old-timers like Tallu Fish will tell you that the stories were often marked by ruthlessness. It was in the clubhouse that J. P. Morgan is said to have described how he purchased for $3.50 apiece several thousand Hall's rifles which had been condemned by the government and resold them at $22 each to General Fremont's army in St. Louis. When fired, the rifles blew the thumbs off the soldiers. But Morgan demanded and got the full purchase price for them, though they were condemned a second time and never used. But sometimes the members turned their attention to lighter topics—when their wives asked for money for shrubbery, six club members put up $5000 apiece in stakes at the poker table to transform the village into a veritable garden.

History was made on Jekyll on at least two occasions. In January, 1915, when the first transcontinental telephone call was made, Theodore N. Vail, president of the American Telephone and Telegraph Company was recuperating from a leg injury on the island. A thousand miles of extra telephone cable was laid to Jekyll Island to enable Vail to participate in this historic first telephone call. Alexander Graham Bell was in New York, Thomas Watson was in San Francisco, and President Woodrow Wilson was on the line in Washington. When the President's time to speak came, he addressed Mr. Vail first.

"Hello, Mr. Vail," said the President.

"Who is this?" Vail answered.

"This is the President," Wilson replied. "I've just been speaking across the continent."

"Oh yes," Vail responded, completing one of the briefest telephone calls in history.

Probably the most important single event in Jekyll's history occurred in 1910, three years after J. P. Morgan had written his personal check for $67 million to the U. S. Government to avert the panic of 1907. Connecticut's Nelson Aldrich was assigned to head a committee to study revisions in the state banking statutes which would prevent future panics. He called four men and asked them to meet him on a remote train platform in Jersey City with their bags packed. At the platform, Aldrich swore the men to silence and told them to address each other only by their first names. He then hurried them into a private car where every precaution was taken to keep the train crew from recognizing them.

Two days later they arrived at Jekyll and for the next ten days they studied the existing bank laws. The five men came to be known as Wall Street's "First Name Club." Besides Aldrich, they were: Frank Vanderlip, president of the National Bank, Henry Davison, right-hand man to the elder J. P. Morgan, Paul Warburg, of Kuhn, Loeb and Co., and Abram P. Andrew, assistant Secretary of the Treasury. Their report was destined to become the Federal Reserve Bank Act. The room in the rambling, gingerbread pink and white hotel where the act was forged is used as a lounge by tourists today.

But Jekyll was not without its personal tragedies. The strangest is probably that of Bayard Brown, an ebullient young millionaire who was engaged to one of New York's most coveted debutantes. For their honeymoon cottage, he built a grandiose house overlooking the Marshes of Glynn, but he was literally left at the altar. His fiancée ran off with another man.

Heartbroken, the young millionaire sailed off in his yacht and, at the age of thirty-seven, became a port bound yachtsman, with his yacht anchored in the harbor at Essex, England. Here it stayed at anchor for thirty-six years, its crew waiting in full readiness for an order to put to sea, while its captain lived the life of a recluse. When the order finally came, it was to carry Brown's body back to the United States for burial.

What gallant Tallu Fish calls Jekyll's glamour era ended as abruptly as it began. Early in April 1942, a German submarine was sighted off the coast of the island. The Coast Guard was concerned. On Jekyll were men representing most of the financial might of the country. President Roosevelt was so advised and he immediately dispatched General George S. Patton to the island to close the club. When Patton, pearl-handled revolvers gleaming at his hip, explained the imminent danger to the club, the members returned to their rooms and cottages, packed hurriedly and left the island that night. Doors were left standing open and clothes were left in some of the closets. The club register, now in the hotel library, shows General Patton and his wife as the last people to sign the official guest book.

JEKYLL ISLAND

The old hotel is open again and the rates are low. Young people lounge in the wicker rockers on the porch or gather at the shell-shaped pool to watch turkeys stalk the grounds and the deer flitting through the moss hung oaks. The island which once regarded all outsiders as strangers today knows no stranger.

12

Cumberland, Ossabaw, and Wassaw

THE THREATENED WILDERNESS

The vast, shimmering reaches of emerald marshes, restoring the cramped heart's sense of infinity . . . the profound mystery of the ancient, tortured, moss-shrouded oak forests . . . the wild horses prancing through sea oats on the majestic dunes . . . dazzling flocks of gulls soaring with sea liberty . . . the virgin beaches and the surf, thundering with the rhythm of eternity, the sense of wonder, of abandon and ecstasy as the severed, squandered self regains its innocence, its wholeness, and its identity with nature.

These, the special properties of the sea islands, were a closely guarded secret of the spirit until recently when they became one of the shrinking arenas where the final scenes of the great American drama are being played out—the conflict between the developers and the conservationists.

When Charles Fraser, developer of Hilton Head, bought a fifth of Cumberland Island, the largest and most spectacularly beautiful of the Georgia sea islands, it became a rallying point for the scattered and divergent island owners—heirs of great families like the Carnegies, the Candlers, the Torreys, and the Parsons, who finally realized that to save the wilderness they cherished they would have to relinquish it, often at a wrenching personal sacrifice, to whatever organizations and institutions there were which had the power and the resources to preserve them.

The owners of Cumberland—the descendants of Thomas Carnegie, the Pittsburgh steel magnate, of Asa Candler, the Coca-Cola baron, and a single Negro, Bob Rischarde, had a profound, almost mystical feeling for the island, for its rich and troubled history, its storied ruins, its infinite marshes, torn by golden streams, its teeming wildlife and its blazing eighteen-mile beach, blessed by soaring, shimmering white flocks of rare sea birds.

A few visitors knew it through Grey Field, the old Carnegie estate, which one of the heirs, "Rick" Ferguson, has converted into an inn. Here, in great high-ceilinged, beamed rooms, amid photographs of the clan in stiff Gay Nineties collars, musty family albums, and heavy, rococo furnishings, they can savor the fading opulence of another era, the ghostly reign of the robber barons. Guided by Ferguson, a lithe, soft-spoken, knowledgeable Renaissance man, they can explore Cumberland's rich and varied history, the grass grown mounds of the Timucuran Indians and the site of a mission built by the Spanish Jesuits when the island was named San Pedro—it was renamed Cumberland at the request of Tomochichi's nephew Toonahowie after the thirteen-year-old Duke of Cumberland

presented him with a gold watch, a symbol of the fast friendship they formed on his visit, with Oglethorpe, to the English
court. Beside a sweep of golden marsh, guarded by a gnarled
and venerable oak, they can discover the little tabby-walled
cemetery which cloisters the tombstones of the Revolutionary
era—General Lighthorse Harry Lee, who died on the island,
and General Nathaniel Greene's widow, Catherine Miller, the
legendary beauty who reigned over Dungeness, an im-
mense four-storied mansion known for its hospitality throughout the fledgling nation. "She was possessed of real talent
and exalted virtue," says the faded inscription on the tombstone of Catherine Miller. She was once the envied ballroom
partner of George Washington and Mad Anthony Wayne,
the ingenious hostess who, while entertaining a guest, Eli
Whitney, offered him a brush to flick the lint from his uncom-
pleted model of the cotton gin and thus completed the inven-
tion of the machine that was to govern the troubled destiny
of the South for a century.

Guests can roam among rows of ghostly brick chimneys,
stark remnants of Cumberland's golden era of sea-island cotton. These are the chimneys of the slave cabins which were
burned after the Civil War by their embittered owner, a
planter named Stafford, who drove his slaves like cattle to
the north end of the island where they lived off the earth in
little palmetto lean-tos and stole across the creek to tiny
Hush-Yo-Mouth Island to shout and sing in the elemental,
impassioned religious rites that sustained them.

They can visit the majestic ruins of another Dungeness—
the towering, turreted, improbable Scotch castle which
Thomas Carnegie built as a final, monumental rebuke to the
exclusive Jekyll Island club and christened with the vener-

able name first brought to Cumberland by Oglethorpe who bestowed it on the little hunting lodge he built when Fort Andrew was his southernmost outpost against the Spanish in Florida.

And guests can also visit that fifth of the severed island which was sold for development—the vast, shifting desert of dunes torn by spectral trees, dead and twisted live oaks which haunt this unearthly region like a company of black wraiths. They can still fish the brilliant, blue fresh-water lake, visited by the white ibis and the blue heron, and they can drive down the spectacular beach, over tangled carpets of lavender morning glories to an unnamed point, washed by a wild and thundering surf, where the gulls wheel and spin with an abandon that shatters the guarded and defensive spirit with pure ecstasy.

It was the threat to this wilderness, with all its liberating beauty, that finally convinced the scattered owners of Cumberland to offer the island as a national seashore on the strict provision that it remain a wilderness area and an island—no causeway was to violate its remote, insular quality. They did not want Cumberland to become another coastal peninsula. For after all, there is something in the heart that needs an island, something in the human spirit that needs to know, even if one never gets there, that somewhere there is an island. And there is a magic in the journeying itself—the long, slow, gull-encircled ferry voyage out of Fernandina or St. Mary's, with the shore cares diminishing in the ferry's wake and the distant oaks of Cumberland slowly looming like an infinite promise in the distance. And to fly in by air, on one of the Golden Isles' tiny planes, swooping and dipping over the measureless marshes and the sea, is to discover the immutable face of God.

Prodded by the possible rape of Cumberland, the owners of all the undeveloped islands—St. Catherine's, Wassaw, Ossabaw, Little St. Simons, Little Cumberland and Cumberland itself, banded together to form an informal association to preserve their legacy of wilderness. They were led by Clifford and Eleanor West, two owners of Ossabaw, who in 1961 founded the Ossabaw Island Project, converting their enormous pink stucco Mediterranean estate into a spa where creative people of every discipline could do the innovative thinking which the islands nurture in a mysterious and incandescent way.

A public information campaign was launched by Bob Hanie, a young man who returned from a teaching stint at an English school on the slopes of Mount Kilimanjaro to find his native country so appallingly disfigured by man's vulgar neon and plastic concept of progress that he launched the Georgia Conservancy, then took the reins of the Georgia Natural Areas Council to preserve the state's vanishing wilderness. He regards nature as a feast, a celebration, and one seldom hears him speak of conservation. He uses instead the word *aduntusan*, a Cherokee word meaning expanded life and spirit, a concept for which Americans have no word.

Behind them all was a new Jeremiah, Dr. Eugene Odum, of the University of Georgia, trying to persuade a heedless, blind, and voracious generation devoted to a shortsighted and ultimately disastrous concept of progress that there must be a master plan for the islands, a system of zoning that would preserve St. Catherine's for archaeological research, Sapelo as a research park, Ossabaw as a center of intellectual inquiry and creativity, and Cumberland as a national seashore. No one understood better than he that it was already seven minutes to midnight on the ecological clock, that man was already an endangered species, and the islands, with their geological secrets, archaeological treasures, rare wildlife, and unique ecology, held many of the answers to the vital questions of our geological origins, the evolution of man, and the intricate systems of dependencies that determine the quality of man's environment, answers to the mysteries which ultimately will determine man's future life on earth.

These were the spokesmen of the new doctrine which the coastal Indians understood instinctively—that the environment over which man has ruled with such a wanton and voracious hand is in truth the source of his being. It was powerfully presented to Atlanta's power structure in a film written by Eleanor West and Dr. Odum and filmed by Clifford West, a consummate film artist whose sensitive profiles of artists like Harry Bertoia and Edvard Munch have been premiered at the Guggenheim Museum and the Smithsonian and have earned him the Golden Eagle award from CINE.

Most of the audience, who had seen the islands only from the cloistered reaches of Sea Island, Jekyll, or Hilton Head, now saw them, on film, in all their wild, spontaneous, and shattering beauty. It was a deeply moving and disturbing experience for many of them, this select body of movers and shakers and builders, and while they discussed it over sherry and cheese on the columned portico of the Atlanta Memorial Arts Center, few of them realized that the auditorium, the only place appropriate for so discriminating a power structure, had been rented at a cost of $100 by Bob Rischarde, owner of a tiny half-acre on Cumberland, a man with such a profound and joyous reverence for life that he had financed, out of a meager pension, this powerful introduction to a region, not only of the South, but of the human heart which he understood perhaps better than anyone.

Traditionally, the island owners have been wise and sensitive guardians of the legacy that was theirs. Few acres have been wantonly sold to developers. Sapelo, long the property of the Reynolds estate, is now under the aegis of the Georgia State Fish and Game Commission and is being used by the University of Georgia Marine Institute as a research park. Tiny Egg Island is now safely in the hands of the Georgia Conservancy, and Wassaw, which had been threatened by burgeoning Savannah, has been sold by the Parsons family to the Nature Conservancy.

In one of Wassaw's rambling clapboard houses—houses distinguished by the intricate carved woodwork of men who devoted their leisure to the crafts—one can see in the family logs the extraordinary feeling of the generations for this incredibly beautiful little island. The logs are filled with thoughtful ruminations on Wassaw's history—on the Negro planter, son of a Sunbury aristocrat and an African slave, who lived with his own slaves in bitter seclusion on Little Wassaw, and the tragedy of the Liberty County slaves, two or three hundred of them, who were shipped to the island in 1846 to escape a cholera epidemic. "And so," wrote one of the chroniclers, "those people with the same love of life and family that we have have landed on their hopeless quest for safety, nearly all destined to suffer the torments of the plague with inadequate shelter, nursing and food and most of them doomed to die and add bereavement to the sufferings of the wretched survivors . . ."

Here, in these musty volumes, are recorded a trip to an Indian mound on St. Catherine's Island which yielded "a pot-

tery jug broken and a dozen shell beads," and a visit to
Wilmington Island "to see a barbecue of a whole ox and a
shout by the negroes . . . after the negroes had stripped bare
the bones of the ox some of them played around with the
big bones over their shoulders, like cudgels of primitive days
and it seemed pretty barbaric."

Here are chronicled the day to day events, picnics and
crabbing, hunting and fishing, dinners of Rhine wine, venison
and broiled teal duck, a honeymoon—"no other place offers
young lovers so complete a world unto themselves"—and
the anguish over the death of a brother.

> There came a time when grief no longer veiled
> The beauty of the scenes that spoke to me of him
> And then the cheerful memory of his dear self
> Companioned me in all my walks
> Through wood, by marsh or pond or beach . . .

And here too, prophetically, are penned these words:

> To those who after us shall carry on
> No such Wassaw life can be as ours has been
> Unless each to the other gives first thought
> And giving all, receives all and even more than gives
> Thus it was with us.

The owners of Ossabaw have a similar feeling for their
magnificent island, larger than Bermuda, which traces its title
back to the first property transfer in Georgia when Oglethorpe landed at Yamacraw Bluff and struck a bargain with
Tomochichi that delivered the mainland into the hands of the
English and preserved Ossabaw, St. Catherine's, and Sapelo
as hunting islands for the Creek Indians. This was one of the

islands for which Mary Bosomworth fought the long and bitter legal battle which was finally settled in 1760. Before the Revolution, the title passed to John Morel, a fiery patriot who rallied to the cause of the Boston Tea Party with 500 barrels of rice and as an officer in the Revolution used this island as a meeting point for the revolutionaries. Morel set out the stately avenue of oaks which still stands, like a vaulted cathedral, on Ossabaw, but this, and the slave cabins are all that remain of what was one of the great coastal empires, a vast indigo plantation peopled by hundreds of slaves who worked as lumbering crews, field hands, dye workers, and toiled on its docks and wharves. The three Morel estates, North End Place, Middle Place, and South End are gone now, but the legends remain of their hunt clubs, their boating clubs, their roistering horse races and the Morel candles, molded in an annual ritual, which blazed in the chandeliers and wall sconces and illumined the family chapel. The Morels, who prospered on the institution of slavery, abolished it before the war and introduced the wage system on Ossabaw. But by the summer of 1863 the island was occupied by Union troops, the fallow fields were overgrown and only old Prince was left to tell the stories of the lavish days when the aristocracy of London, Philadelphia, Charleston, and Savannah gathered on the island to shoot ducks in the fresh-water ponds and hunt deer in the climax forests.

Today a new aristocracy of students, artists, scientists, and scholars people the rambling pink stucco mansion now owned by Eleanor and Clifford West, who have placed Ossabaw under a consortium of Georgia colleges and universities as the nation's first Institute of Human Ecology, an institute devoted to developing human potential in both the humanities and the sciences. In the evenings they take their cocktails before a blazing fireplace whose massive mantel and chimney were brought to the coast in sailing vessels in the early days of the colony. The conversation is crisp and lively, a rapid crossfire between writers, poets, painters, and scholars, that continues over dinner at the long, princely table, and dwindles only in the evening when guests settle in the deep sofas to watch one of Clifford West's films or listen to the readings of a visiting poet.

During the day, fellows may be working at easels or pianos in the slave quarters that have been converted into studios. Or they may set out in jeeps through the avenue of live oaks to explore the island's hundred miles of unpaved roads, to discover the egret rookery, the fresh-water lake visited by flocks of migratory ducks, and the majestic live oak, six centuries old, which stands thirty feet in circumference—the most ancient and venerable of all the hoary guardians of the Georgia sea islands.

Among the wildlife, the donkeys jousting at dusk, the streams of piglets, the fawns flitting through the wild dogwood, the suckling calves and wild horses, the sudden flight of ibis and heron, the visitor is humbled and moved by a sense of his place in nature, of the infinite extent of his relationships with the creatures of this earth and the land which sustains them.

Suddenly his jaded senses are restored. He finds himself regaining his tactile senses, running his hands over the abrasive oyster shells of a tabby wall, or the bark of a veiled live oak. He savors the tang of fennel or a bay leaf plucked from a branch. He can smell again the rich, funky, fertile marshes, the hypnotic honeysuckle, like incense in these virgin forests, and the clean, heady, healing scent of unsullied air. And on the beaches, torn with shimmering inlets and an unearthly forest of lifeless trees, gnarled and molded into an infinitely beautiful sculpture, he regains his sense of mystery.

The creative experience of Ossabaw has yielded so many books, paintings, musical compositions and archaeological treasures that the Wests are now planning three museums on the island to display them—one devoted to creative works, one to nature, ecology, and archaeology, and one to coastal histories.

But perhaps the richest harvest of the island experience is in the essence of human life, in something as intangible and indescribable as the morning mist over the marshes or the cry of the pixilated woodpecker they call the Lord God. It is something one feels in the presence of Bob Rischarde, a man who has learned that "the enormous, invulnerable beauty of things is the face of God" and lives gladly in its presence, ready to die without grief or fear knowing that it will survive him.

Rischarde lives like Thoreau on Cumberland in a spare, bright red house which he calls the Red Barn, a house of enormous dignity which reflects his respect for the grace and utility of the implements of his household. His pots and pans are hung neatly on a kitchen wall. The shelves are lined with his herbs. His highly polished boots stand, proud and erect, on a window ledge in a room furnished with two austere beds; his bar is stocked with Noilly Prat and fine cocktail glasses, and his silver coffee urn and white cups and saucers are set neatly on a little chrome table. A turtle shell is placed symbolically by the fireside, and the long shelf on which he takes his meals is set beneath the window which catches the full glory of the Cumberland sunset.

On the wall are hung his two most cherished documents— his lovely wife Adele's master's degree in speech therapy from New York University and his deed to Cumberland Island, purchased from a Brunswick Negro who bought it from a former slave in the 1890s.

Outside is a scuppernong arbor—a hand-lettered sign labels it "The Carousel"—from which he makes the fine wines and beers he bottles in Coca-Cola bottles, in deference to the Candlers, and stores in "The Conchshell," his dark, pungently sweet little wine cellar. In another building is his 1949 jeep, the oldest jeep on the island, which stands, stately as a Cadillac, crowned with a red board roof.

The ceremony with which he celebrates the rituals of life is best savored at dinner, an impromptu meal he has assembled, with no air of haste or effort, for Bob Hanie, Sam Candler, who gave up his life as a gentleman farmer to devote himself to conservation, and Jesse Bailey, a cousin of the Sapelo Island clan of Gullahs, who is still muddy from a day in the marshes. The meal begins beneath the oaks, around a little table, with Cutty Sark in frosted glasses, wedges of Camembert and black caviar, served on toast with a sliver of lemon. Rischarde lifts his silver mug in a toast—"to Jesse, you black bastard," and with the first draught of scotch, the distinctions of race, creed, and background vanish, for this is an authentic, aesthetic aristocracy—the lovers of the coastal wilderness.

The song of the katydids rises like a symphony from the marshes, a proud, sweet, musical rebuke to the meanness of lesser, land-locked lives, and the Lord God flits through the trees like a blessing. "The world," says Bob Rischarde, "is such a pretty place."

As the golden day flares and dwindles into dusk, he ruminates on his past, on his forebears—a New Orleans slaveholder named Rischarde and the beautiful housegirl who bore him twelve children, on the gentle grandmother who raised him in Brunswick sustained by the earnings of a beautiful, flamboyant, aunt who ran a bawdyhouse for the white gentry —he still remembers her spirited temper and her rustling silks, purchased from the fine department stores of New York. He recalls his childhood friends at the Episcopal school in Brunswick, men like W. B. DuBois whom he knew at Atlanta Baptist College, his career at Herndon's Barber Shop, where he shone the boots of the gentry so well that they shipped them on to Bermuda when he moved there to become a waiter. As a luggage weigher with Air France he met and knew the famous and the infamous, from Duke Ellington to Lucky Luciano, and he can talk as knowledgeably of the Astors and the Vanderbilts as he does of Jesse's people on Sapelo Island.

His freewheeling intelligence ranges from the folly of wars to the discrimination he has endured from the Camden County rednecks who have tried to run him off the island; from the theatre, the arts, and the music of Duke Ellington to his philosophy of work—"eight months a year is enough for any man"—from man's need for solitude, for silence and beauty to religion—he does not go to church, but each year he paints the abandoned clapboard sanctuary across the way because "I like to do something for God."

He is a mystic, with a profound sense of infinity, who is quite certain he lived on this earth, this Cumberland earth, a thousand years ago. "Why? Because I am so happy," he says, gazing up at the first faint stars, a bald little man in his seventies, barefoot and relaxed in shorts and a neatly pressed shirt. "This is heaven here and now. We're living in it this minute, here on Cumberland Island." And he wants his death celebrated with a cocktail party and three pieces of music—"Claire de Lune," Rubinstein's "Melody in F" and Duke Ellington's "Prelude to a Kiss."

At dinner, which he serves continental style with a green salad first, then a pot roast, stuffed potatoes, broccoli and a side dish of pork, he pours his rich beer, for this is a feast of love, a ritual of the heart. As the blood warms and the toasts grow ribald, the talk goes back to Cumberland, to the magic of watching the moon rise from the shores of Lake Whitney, to the developers who would rape this strange and beautiful wilderness, this heaven he has found on earth, his half acre of eternity in the here and now. As the evening wanes, the symphony of Cumberland subsides and his guests depart, he hands them his Christmas card, a vague, tenuous Chinese brush painting inscribed with the hand-lettered message he and his wife have chosen with such exquisite wisdom.

> By gaining
> Freedom from illusion
> One returns
> To the ultimate.
> —TAO-SHENG

Epilogue

The future of Georgia's coastal islands is uncertain. This is still a debatable land, and the forces which threaten it, unlike the Spanish and the English, the plantation lords and the robber barons, could ultimately destroy the islands, the vast, protective marshlands, and the surrounding waters.

The islands' predators include foreign chemical manufacturers, phosphate miners and heavy industry; developers who now have whole recreation cities on the drawing boards; and the back-country politicians who would squander this irrecoverable legacy on the tawdry commerce of the twentieth century—nightclubs and hamburger stands, filling stations and memorial parks.

The scientists, the new Jeremiahs like Dr. Eugene Odum and Dr. James Henry of the Marine Institute on Sapelo and Bob Hanie of the Georgia Natural Areas Council, recognize the destructiveness of the predators. They understand the unique ecology of the Georgia coast; the facts have been well documented. The ravaged beaches of Savannah with their crumbling sea walls and the deadly foaming waters of the Savannah River speak starkly and tragically of man's infinite power to desecrate and destroy. All too soon the teeming ocean could be devoid of all sea life, the torn and shifting beaches could perish with the new canals and condominiums—they are already shored with plastic at Hilton Head—and the marshes could die with the new highways. And with them would die something of the spirit of man, something vital to his humanity, his capacity for life, his sense of wonder and mystery.

To enter this world, this insular world, is to enter a new dimension. The twentieth century—the world of steel and concrete, of smog and searing noise, of folly and endless corruption, takes on a curious sense of unreality when one makes the island voyage. This is not a journey to be lightly undertaken, for a wilderness island is what one brings to it. It is a confrontation with one's self, and this can be both terrifying and infinitely rewarding. One is apt to lose himself and find that he can never be quite the same again.

He may lose himself to pure ecstasy strolling a deserted beach through flashing clouds of sea birds on Cumberland Island, and on another day, storm-tossed, when the rain is like a whiplash and the surf roars in with a savage fury, he may lose himself in the infinite sorrow of life, in the cry of heart-wrenching poignance washed in from a thousand un-seen shores by the mewing, grieving gulls.

On Cumberland, when one crosses the vast desert of dunes through the dead forest, the gnarled, black, wraith-like oaks which the sand has reclaimed, one comes to an improbable sapphire blue fresh-water lake marked by a wooden cross—during the plantation era the slaves held Easter services here, "Rick" Ferguson will tell you. Beyond the cross, if you fol-low the rolling sandy shores of the lake, is a glade of oaks, a shadowy oasis where the wind in the Spanish moss is the barest murmur of eternity. Here the inlander, visited by fleet, shy fawns and the warbler they call the Lord God, realizes the terrible folly of man's dominion over the birds of the air, over the beasts of the field. Humbled by this rich wilderness, he realizes that only by living in harmony with nature can man live in harmony with himself. The destiny of the wilderness islands lies ultimately in this realization.

Selected Bibliography

Biographical Dictionary of the Franciscans in Spanish Florida and Cuba (1528–1841), in *Franciscan Studies*, Vol. XXI. Paterson, New Jersey, 1940.

BOLTON, HERBERT E. and MARY ROSS, *The Debatable Land.* Berkeley, California, The University of California Press, 1925.

BUTLER, PIERCE, *Mr. Butler's Statement.* Originally prepared in aid of his Professional Counsel. Copy in Margaret Davis Cate Library, St. Simons Island, Georgia.

CANDLER, ALLEN D., comp., *Colonial Records of Georgia.* Atlanta.

CATE, MARGARET DAVIS, *Early Days of Coastal Georgia.* St. Simons Island, Fort Frederica Association, 1955.

Selected Bibliography

CHATELAIN, VERNE E., *The Defenses of Spanish Florida, 1565 to 1763*, Washington, D.C., 1941.

CHURCH, LESLIE F., *Oglethorpe, A Study of Philanthropy in England and Georgia*. London, Epworth Press, 1932.

COLEMAN, KENNETH and SARAH GOBER TEMPLE, *Georgia Journeys, 1732–1754*. Athens, University of Georgia Press, 1961.

COULTER, E. MERTON, *Negro Legislators in Georgia During the Reconstruction Period*. Athens, University of Georgia Press, 1965.

COULTER, E. MERTON, *The Journal of Peter Gordon, 1732–1735*. Athens, University of Georgia Press, 1963.

COULTER, E. MERTON, *Thomas Spalding of Sapelo*. Baton Rouge, University of Louisiana Press, 1941.

COULTER, E. MERTON, *Wormsloe*. Athens, University of Georgia Press, 1955.

CRANE, VERNER W., *The Southern Frontier, 1670–1732*. Ann Arbor, University of Michigan Press, 1929.

DRIVER, LEOTA S., *Fanny Kemble*. Chapel Hill, University of North Carolina Press, 1933.

Drums and Shadows, Survival Studies Among the Georgia Coastal Negroes. Savannah Unit Works Projects Administration, Athens, University of Georgia Press, 1940.

FISH, TALLU, *Once Upon an Island*. Jekyll Island, Georgia, 1959.

FLANDERS, RALPH BETTS, *Plantation Slavery in Georgia*. Cos Cob, Connecticut, John E. Edwards, 1967.

[213]

Selected Bibliography

FORD, ELIZABETH AUSTIN, *Jekyll Island*. Decatur, Georgia, 1960.

GAMBLE, THOMAS, *Savannah Duels and Duellists, 1733–1877*. Savannah, Review Publishing and Printing Company, 1923.

GEORGIA SOCIETY OF THE COLONIAL DAMES OF AMERICA, *Some Early Epitaphs in Georgia*. Durham, North Carolina, The Seaman Printery, Inc., 1924.

GIBBS, HENRY, *Affectionately Yours, Fanny*. London, 1946.

GIBSON, COUNT D., *Sea Islands of Georgia*. Athens, University of Georgia Press, 1948.

HARDEN, WILLIAM, *A History of Savannah and South Georgia*. Chicago and New York, Lewis Publishing Company, 1913.

HOLMGREN, VIRGINIA C., *Hilton Head, A Sea Island Chronicle*. Hilton Head Island, South Carolina, Hilton Head Publishing Company, 1959.

HOWE, GEORGE, *History of the Presbyterian Church in South Carolina*. Columbia, South Carolina, 1870.

KEMBLE, FRANCES ANNE, *Journal of a Residence on a Georgian Plantation in 1838–1839*. New York, Alfred A. Knopf, 1961.

KEMBLE, FRANCES ANNE, *Records of a Girlhood*. New York, 1879.

KEMBLE, FRANCES ANNE, *Records of a Later Life*. New York, Henry Holt and Company, 1882.

LANNING, JOHN TATE, *The Spanish Missions of Georgia*. Chapel Hill, University of North Carolina Press, 1935.

LAWRENCE, ALEXANDER, *A Present for Mr. Lincoln*. Macon, Georgia, The Ardivan Press, 1961.

LOVELL, CAROLINE COUPER, *The Golden Isles of Georgia*. Boston, Little, Brown and Co., 1933.

LOWERY, WOODBURY, *The Spanish Settlements within the Present Limits of the United States, 1513–1561*. New York and London, 1901.

MCCALL, CAPT. HUGH, *The History of Georgia, Containing Brief Sketches of the Most Remarkable Events up to the Present Day (1784)*. Savannah, 1811.

MCPHERSON, ROBERT G., editor, *The Journal of the Earl of Egmont*. Athens, University of Georgia Press, 1962.

MONTGOMERY, SIR ROBERT, *A Discourse Concerning the Design'd Establishment of a New Colony to the South of Carolina*. London, 1717.

PARRISH, LYDIA, *Slave Songs of the Georgia Sea Islands*. New York, Creative Age Press, Inc., 1942.

PERKERSON, MEDORA FIELD, *White Columns in Georgia*. New York, Rinehart, 1952.

PRICE, EUGENIA, *New Moon Rising*. New York, J. B. Lippincott Company, 1969.

PRICE, EUGENIA, *The Beloved Invader*. New York, J. B. Lippincott Company, 1965.

PUCKETT, NEWELL NILES, *Folk Beliefs of the Southern Negro*. Chapel Hill, University of North Carolina Press, 1926.

REESE, TREVOR RICHARD, *Colonial Georgia*. Athens, University of Georgia Press, 1963.

ROSE, WILLIE LEE, *Rehearsal for Reconstruction, the Port Royal Experiment.* New York, Vintage Books, 1967.

SHERMAN, WILLIAM T., *Memoirs of General William T. Sherman, Vol. 11.* New York, D. Appleton and Company, 1875.

STACY, JAMES, *History of the Midway Congregational Church, Liberty County, Georgia.* Newnan, Georgia, 1894.

STEEL, EDWARD M., JR., *T. Butler King of Georgia.* Athens, University of Georgia Press, 1964.

STEVENS, WILLIAM BACON, M.D., *History of Georgia, Vol. 1.* New York, D. Appleton and Company, 1847.

SWANTON, JOHN R., *Early History of the Creek Indians and their Neighbors.* Smithsonian Institution Bureau of American Ethnology Bulletin 73, Washington, D.C., 1922.

TEAL, JOHN AND MILDRED, *Portrait of an Island.* New York, Atheneum, 1964.

Testimony Taken by the Joint Select Committee to Inquire into the Condition of Affairs in the Late Insurrectionary States, Vol. 11. Washington, D.C., 1872.

VANSTORY, BURNETTE, *Georgia's Land of the Golden Isles.* Athens, University of Georgia Press, 1967.

WELLS, TOM HENDERSON, *The Slave Ship Wanderer.* Athens, University of Georgia Press, 1967.

WYLLY, CHARLES SPALDING, *The Seed That Was Sown in the Colony of Georgia: the Harvest and Aftermath, 1740–1870.* New York, 1910.